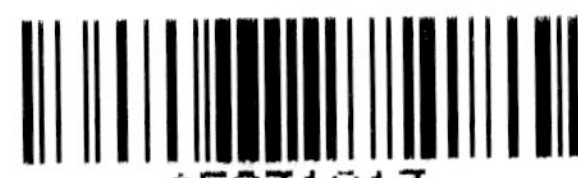

This Book Belongs to:

....

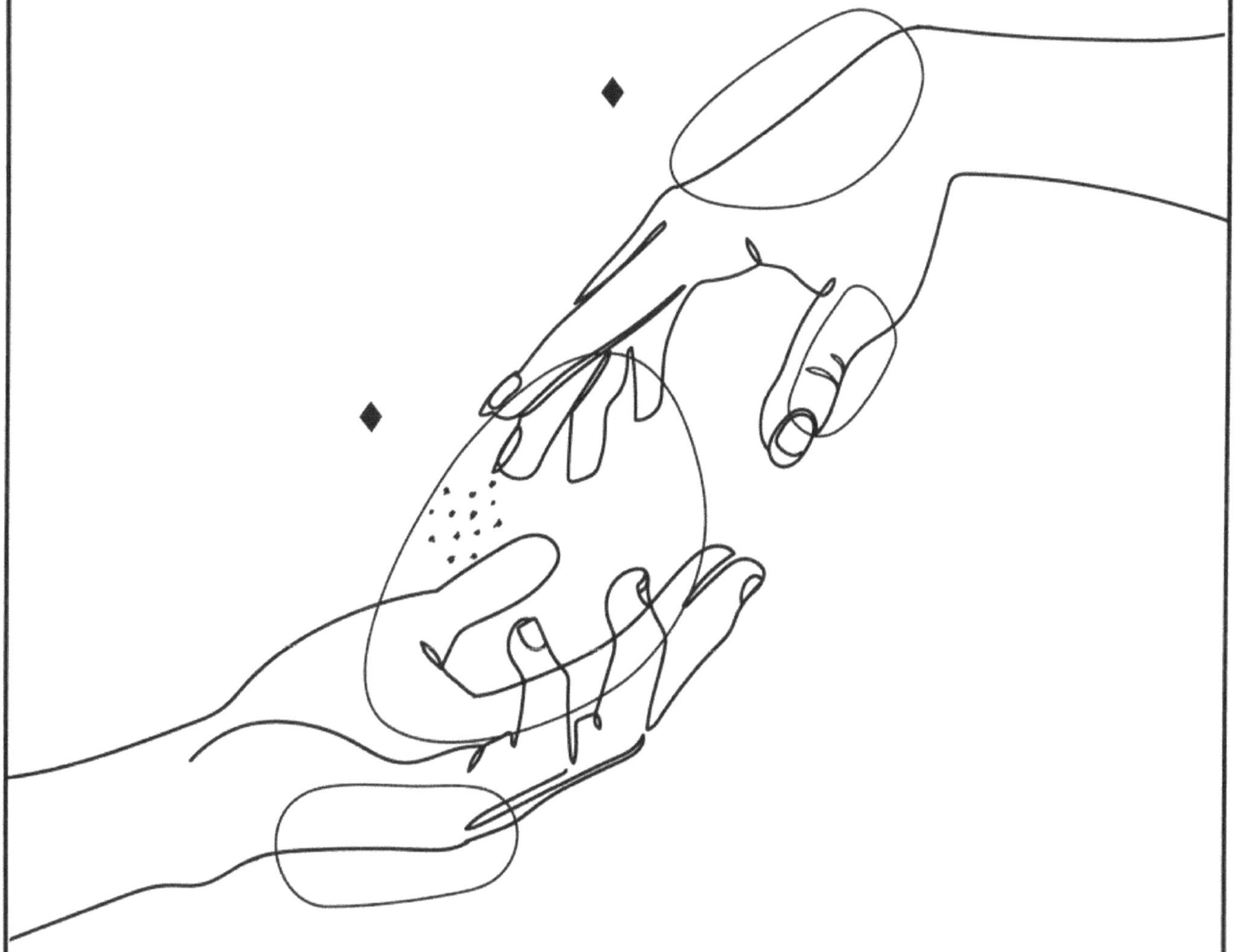

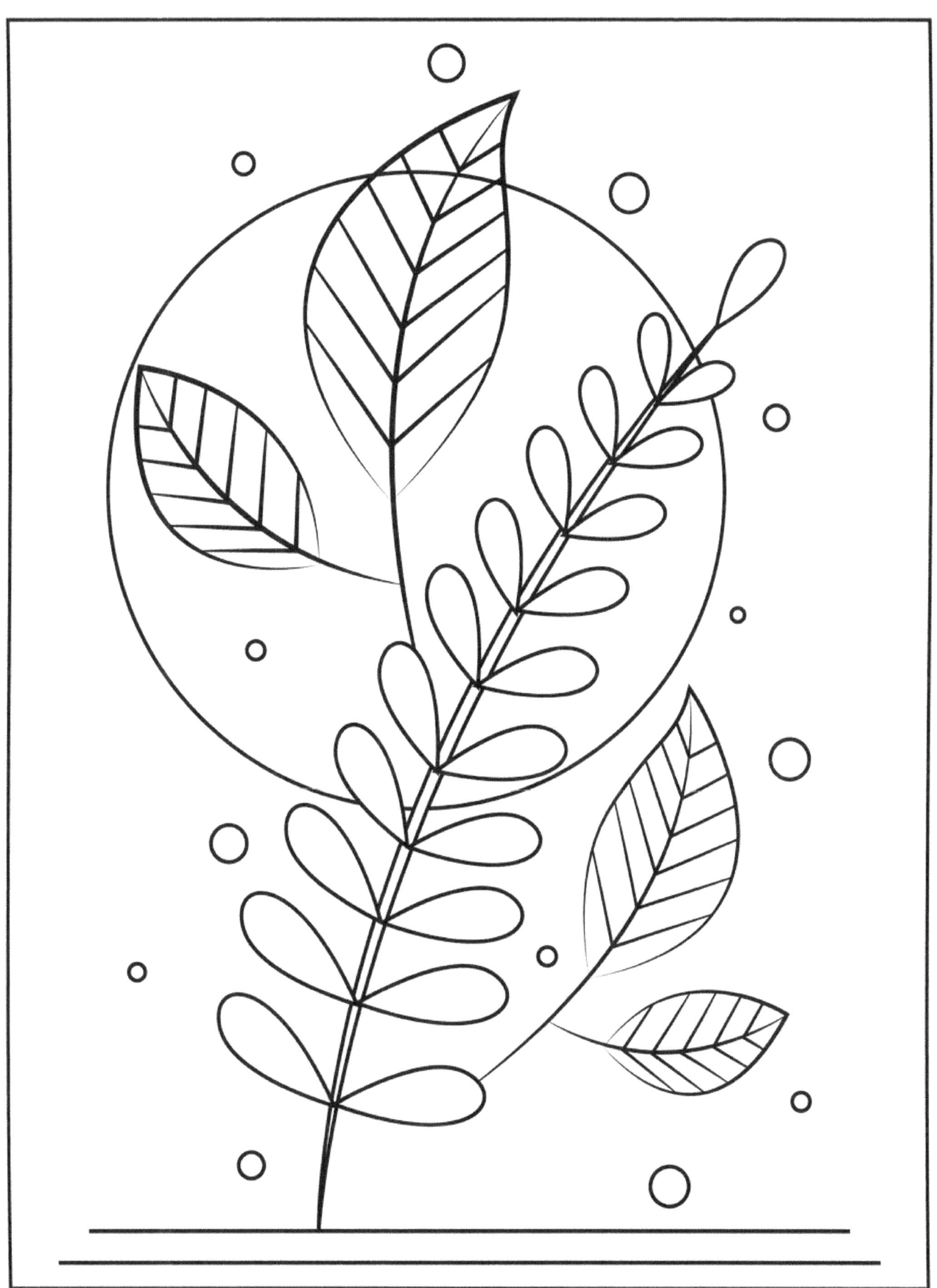

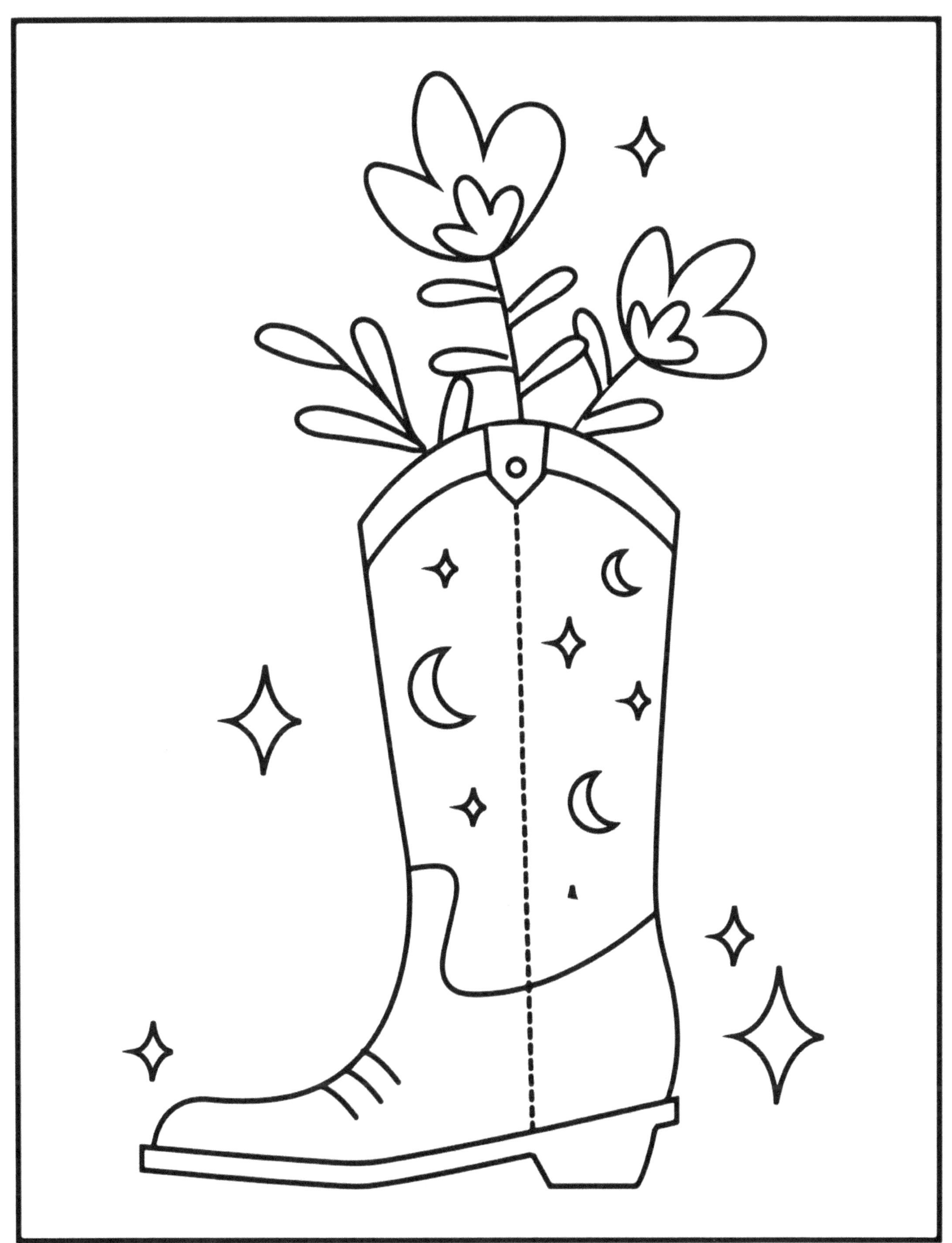

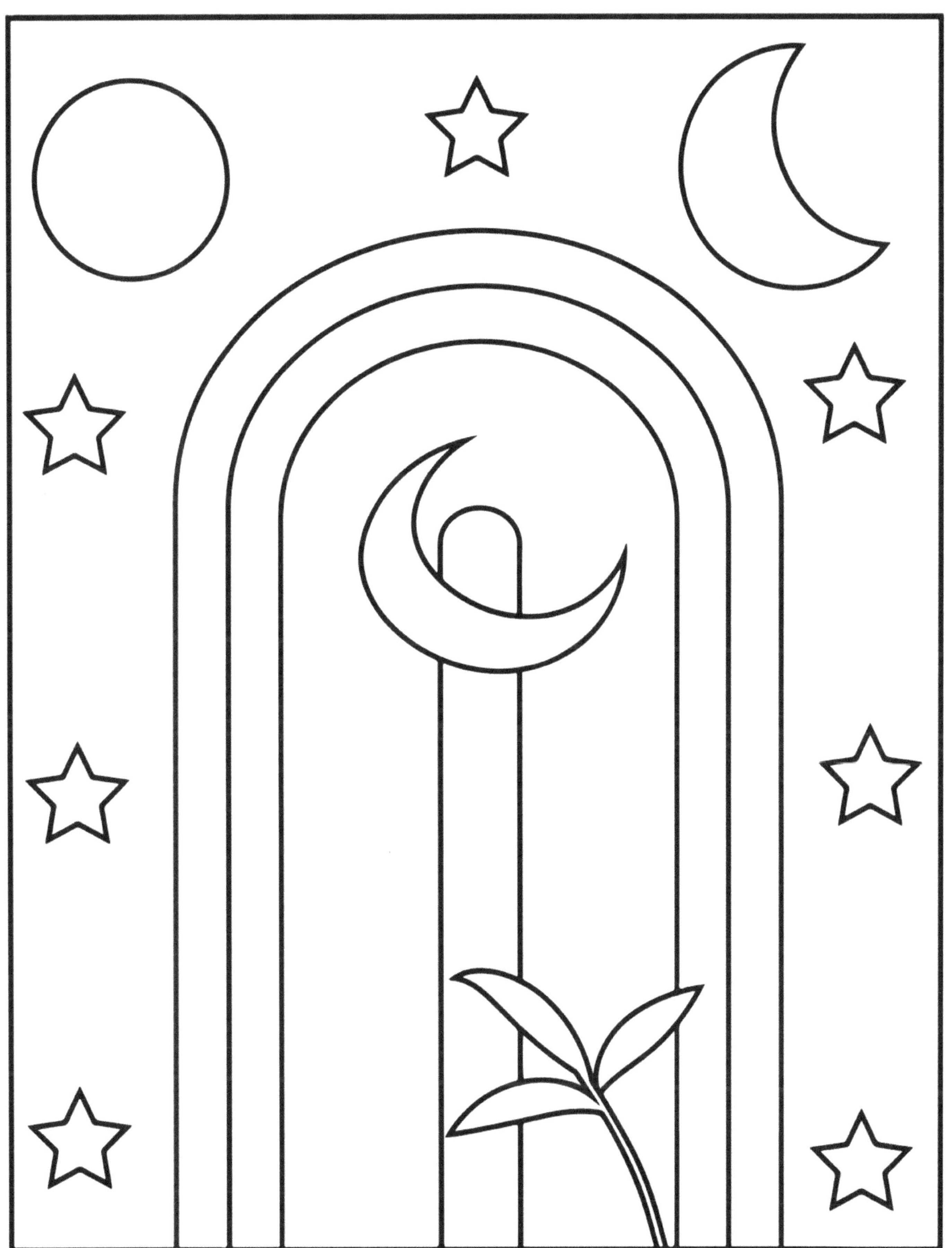

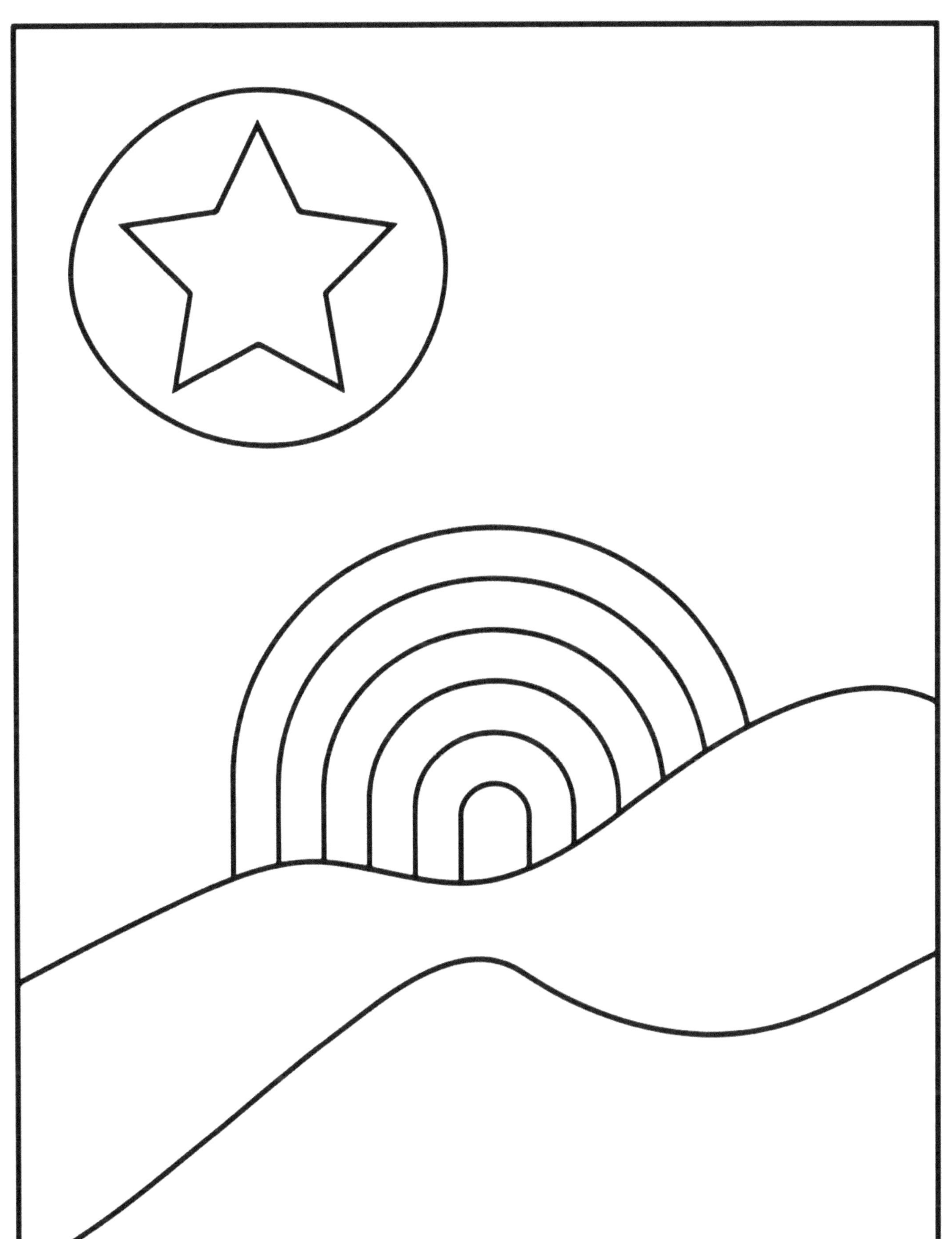

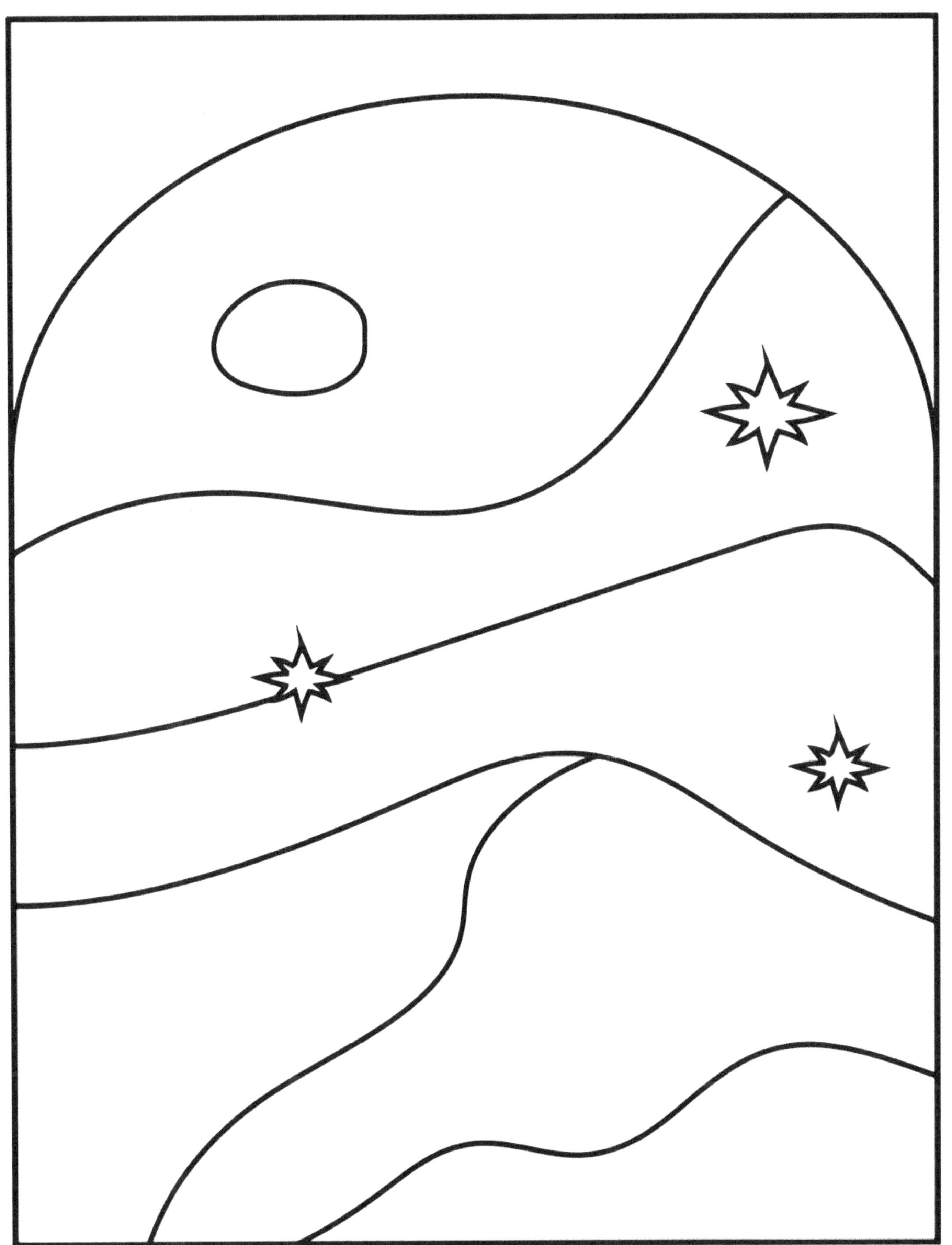

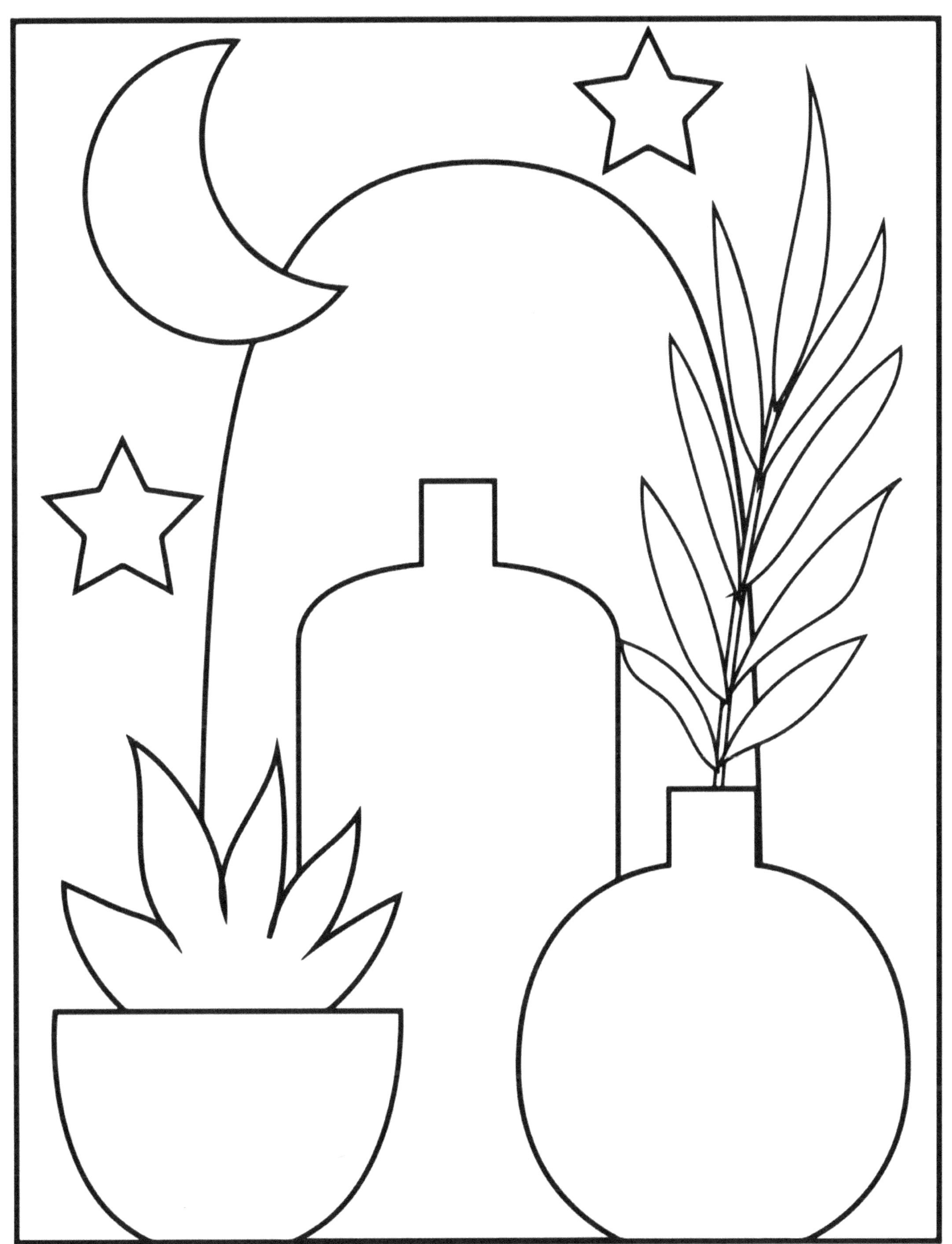

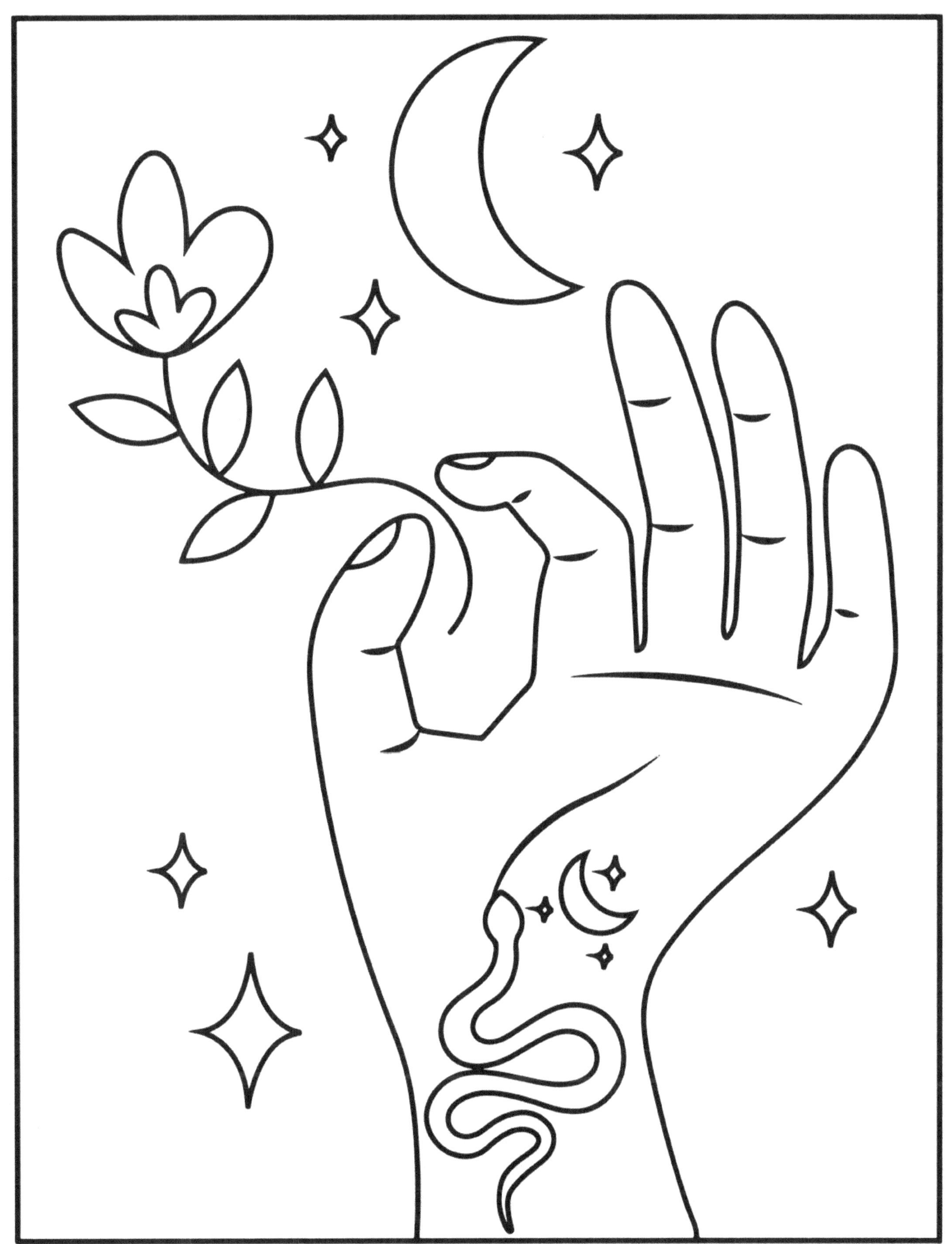

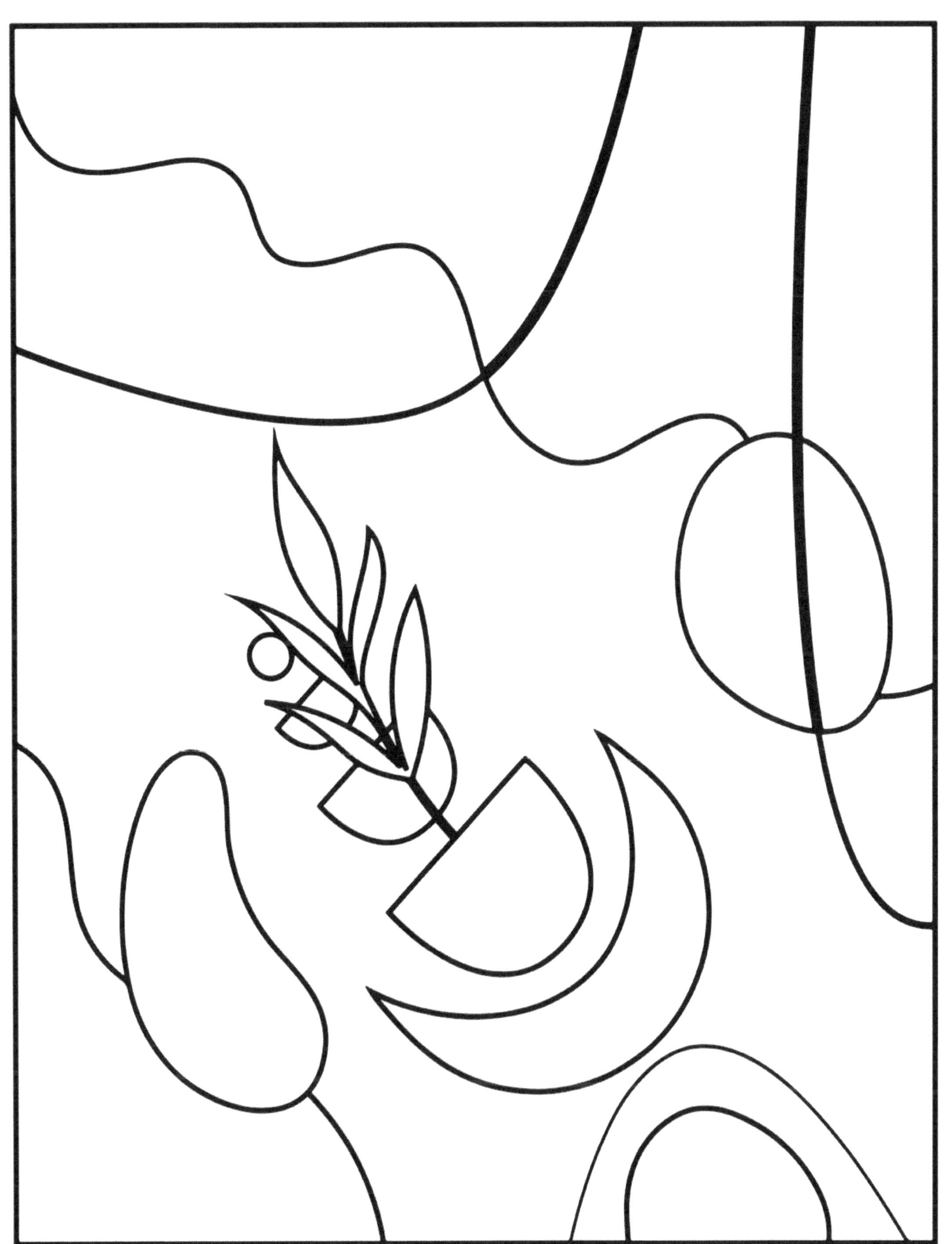

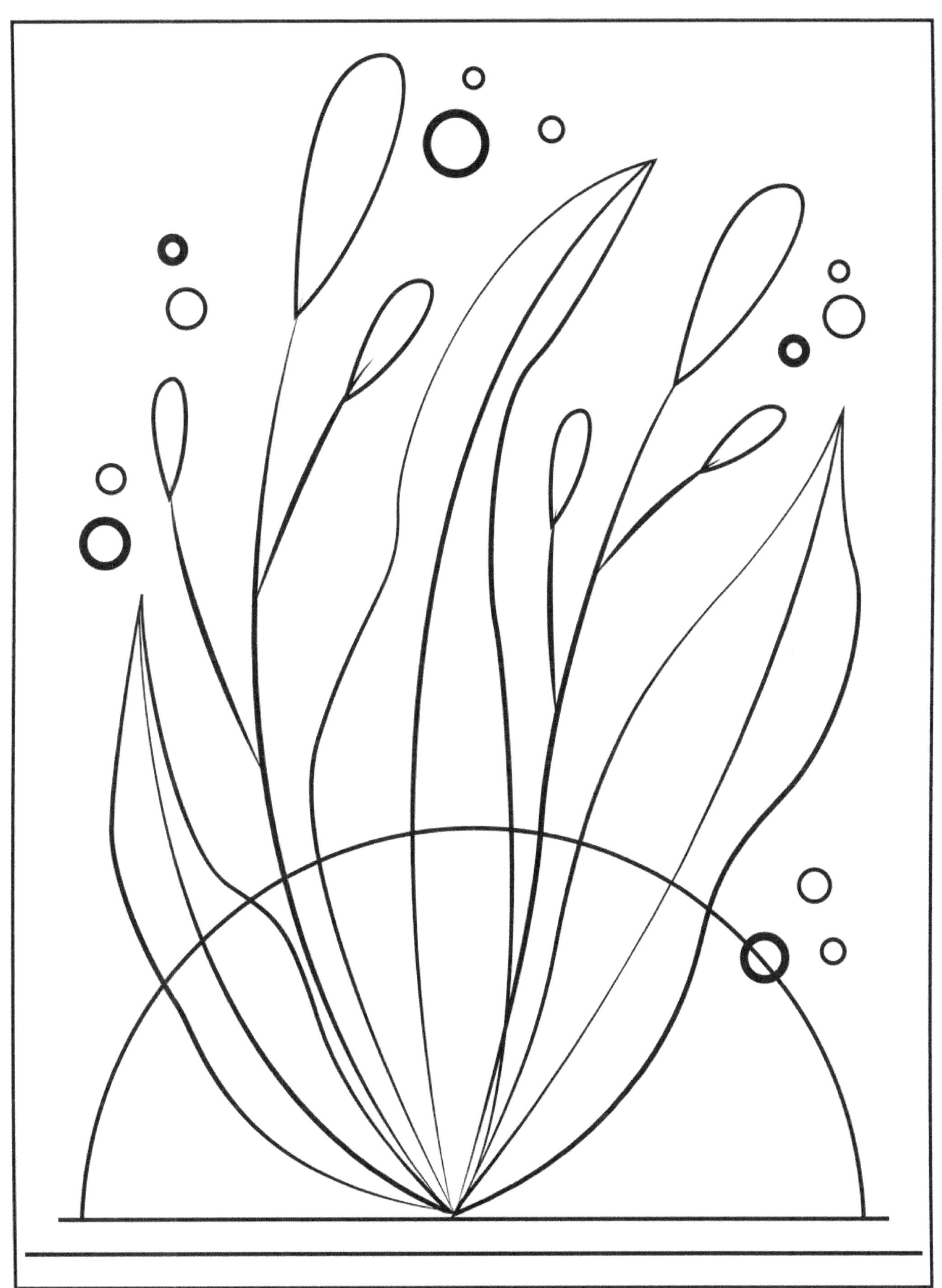

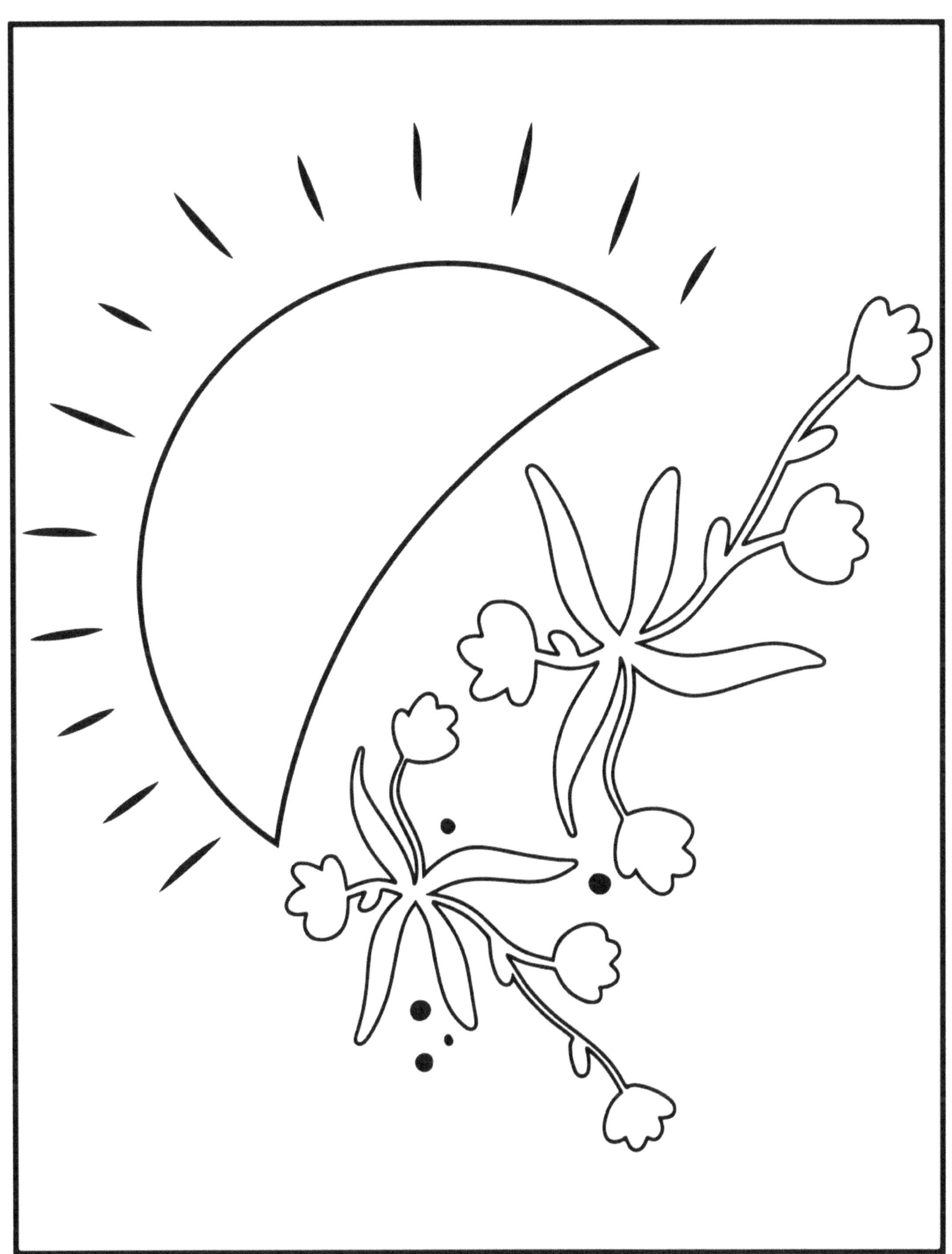

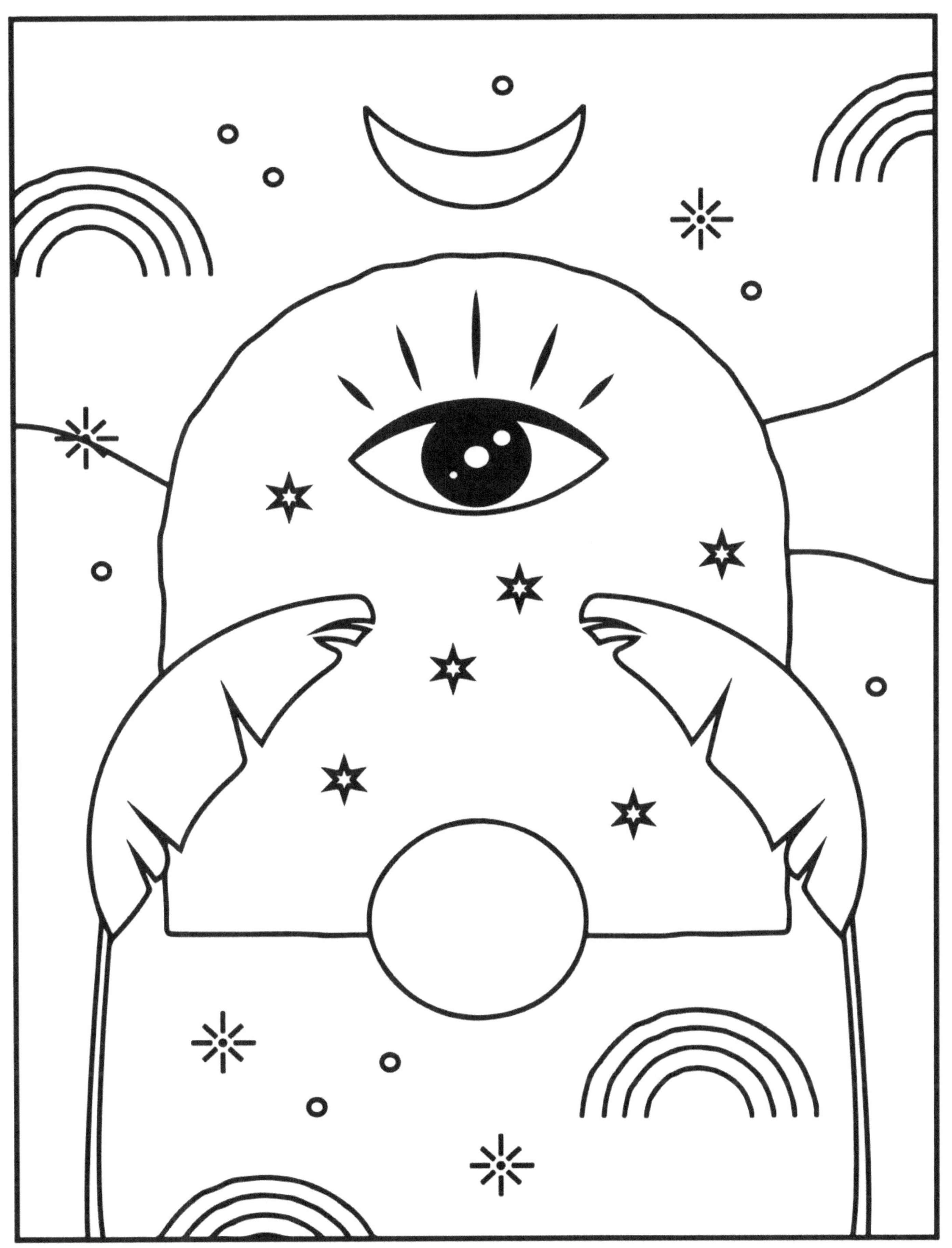

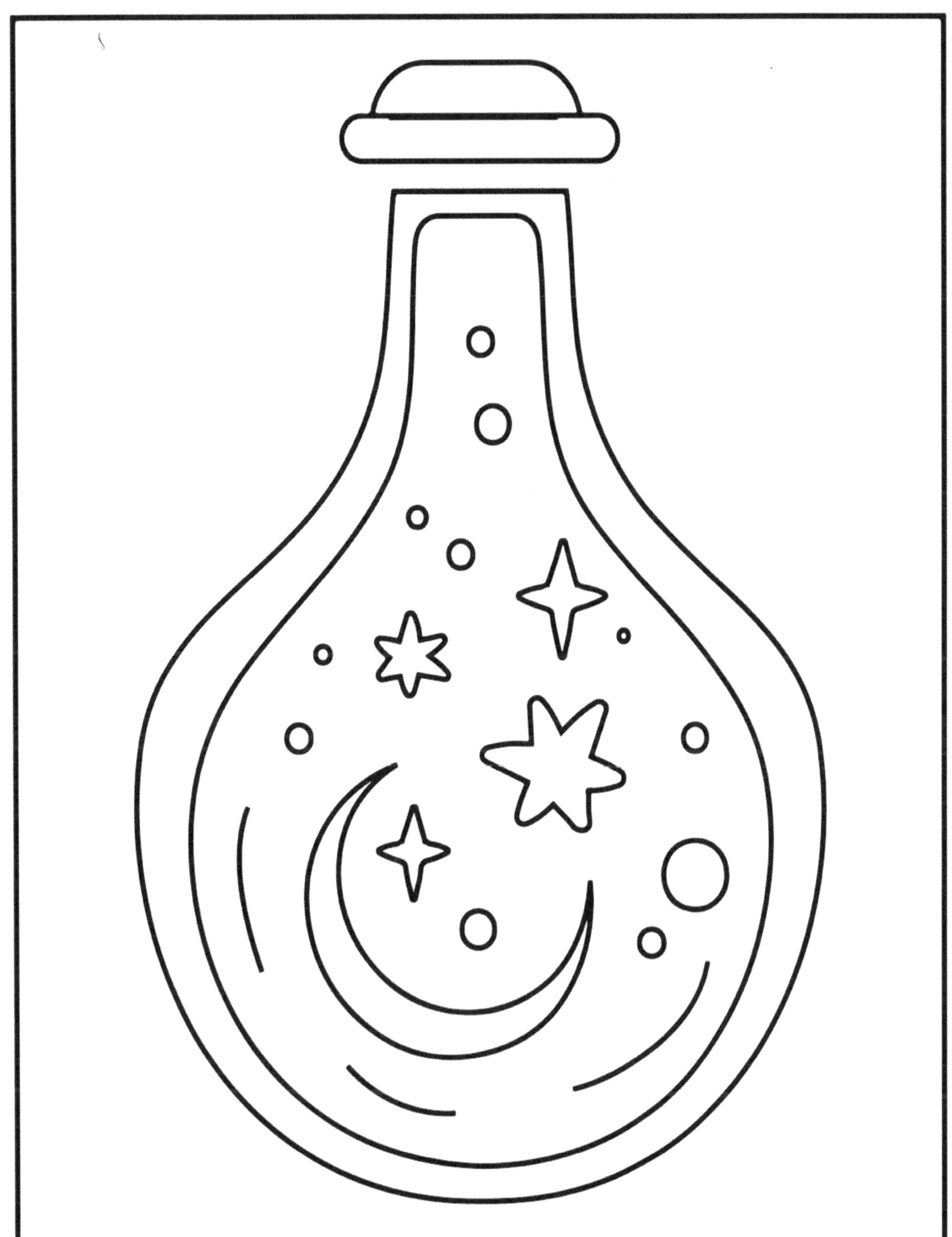

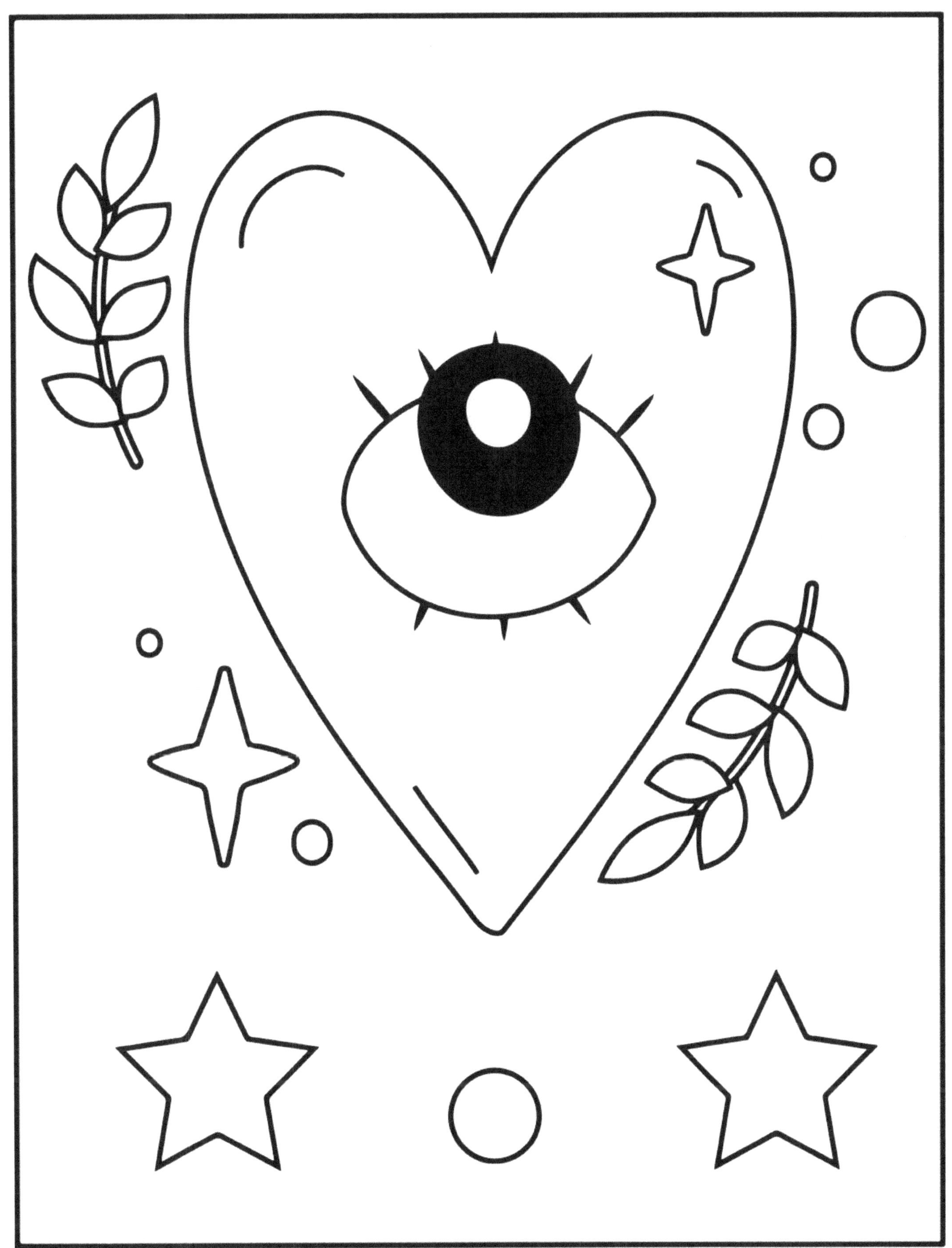

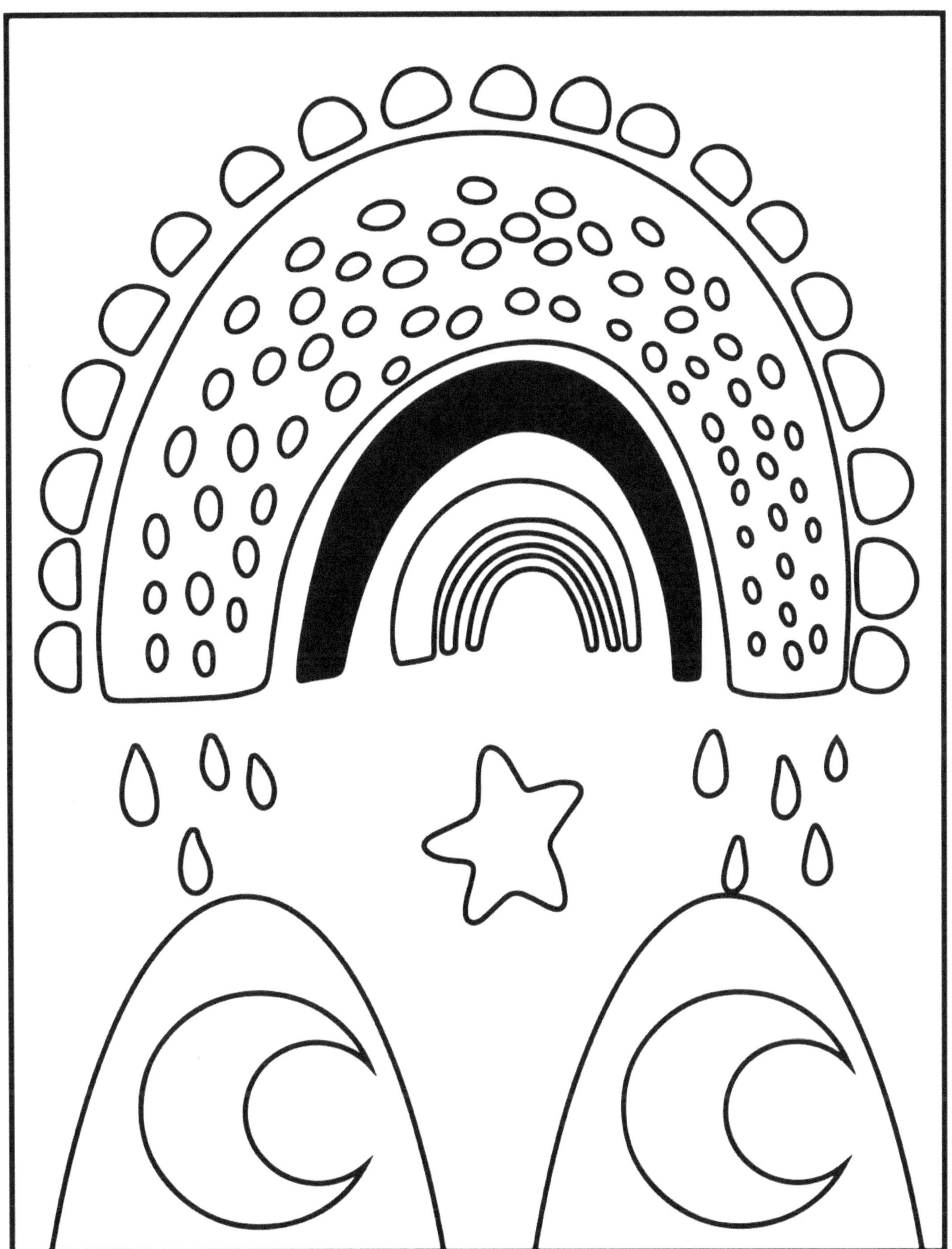

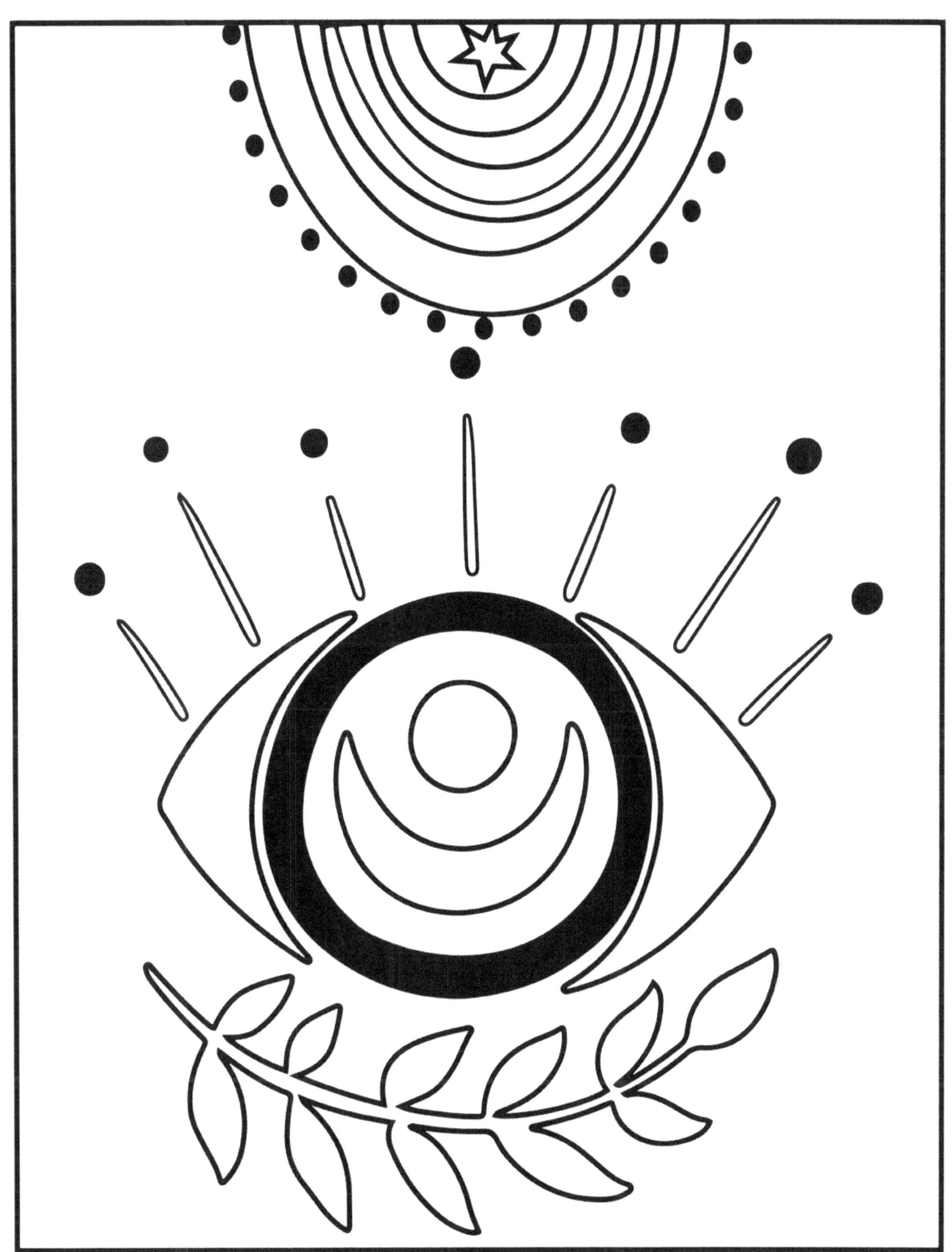

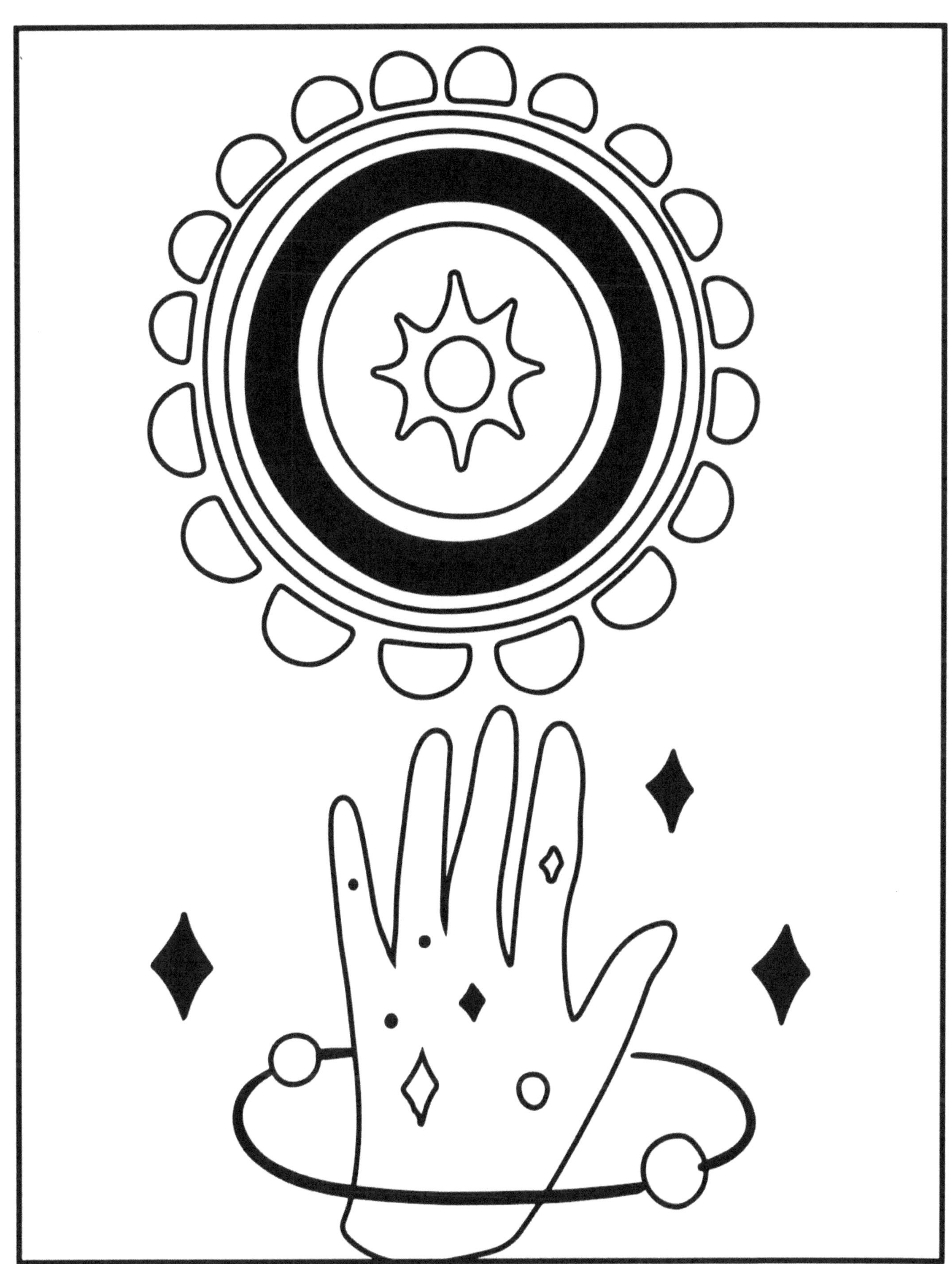

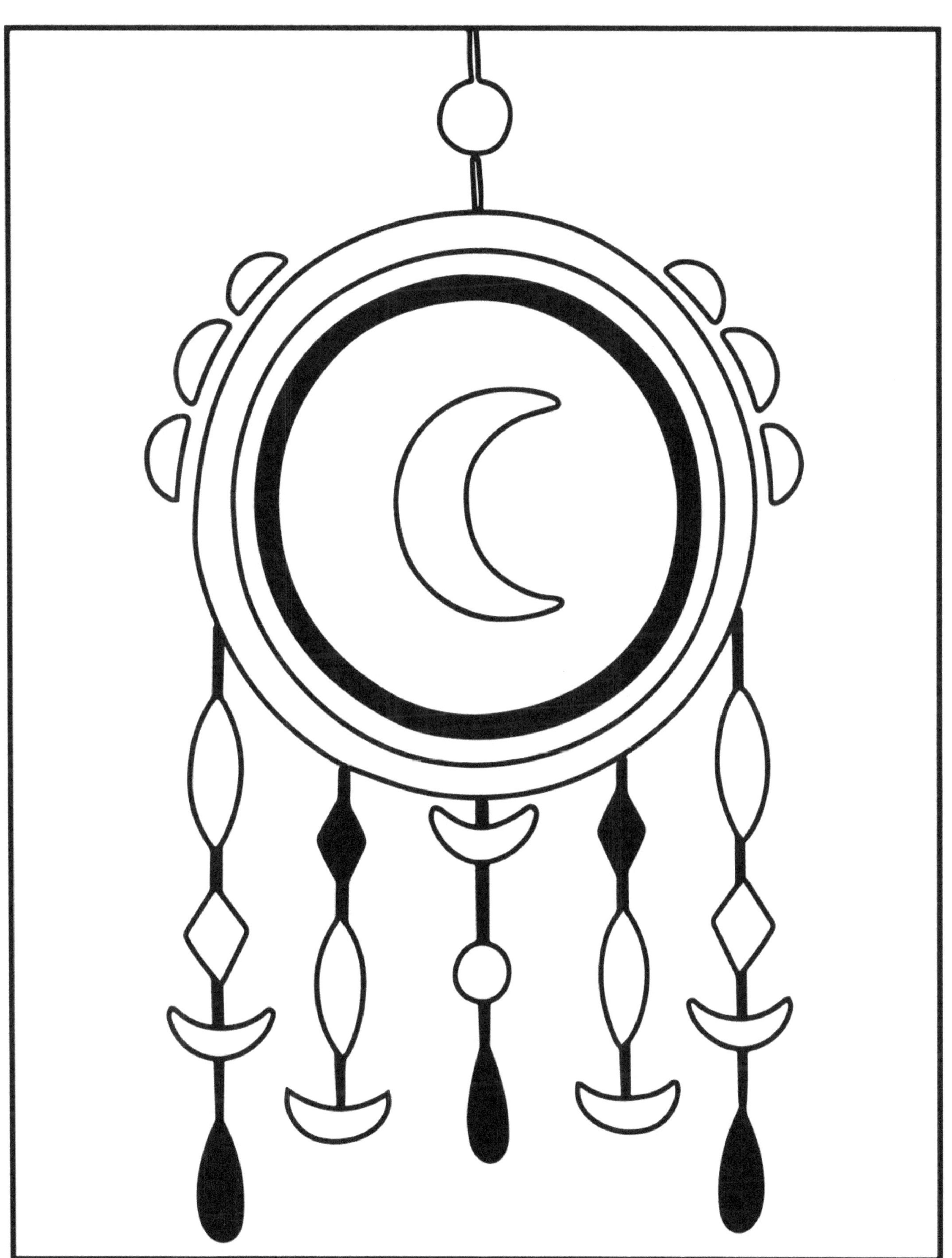

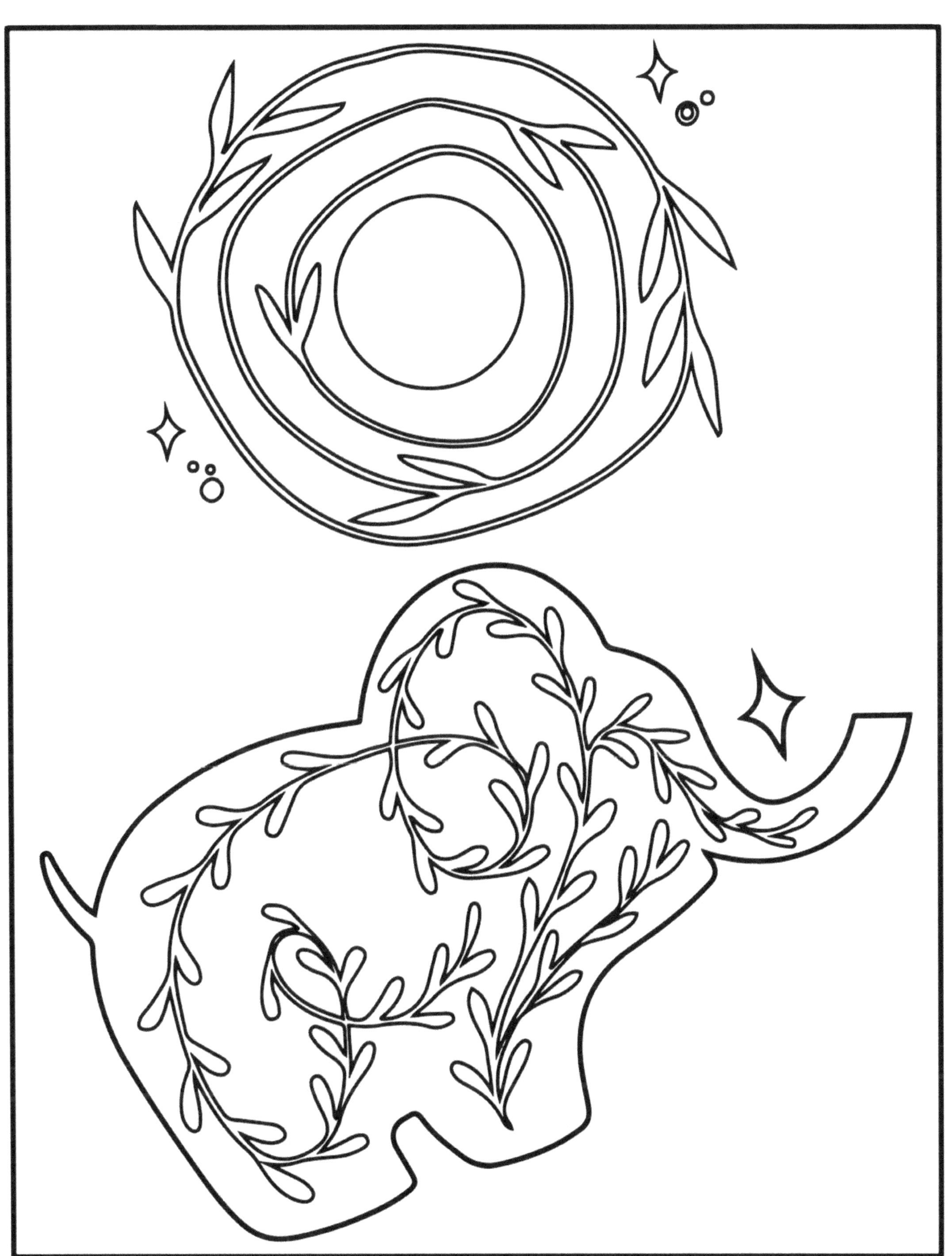

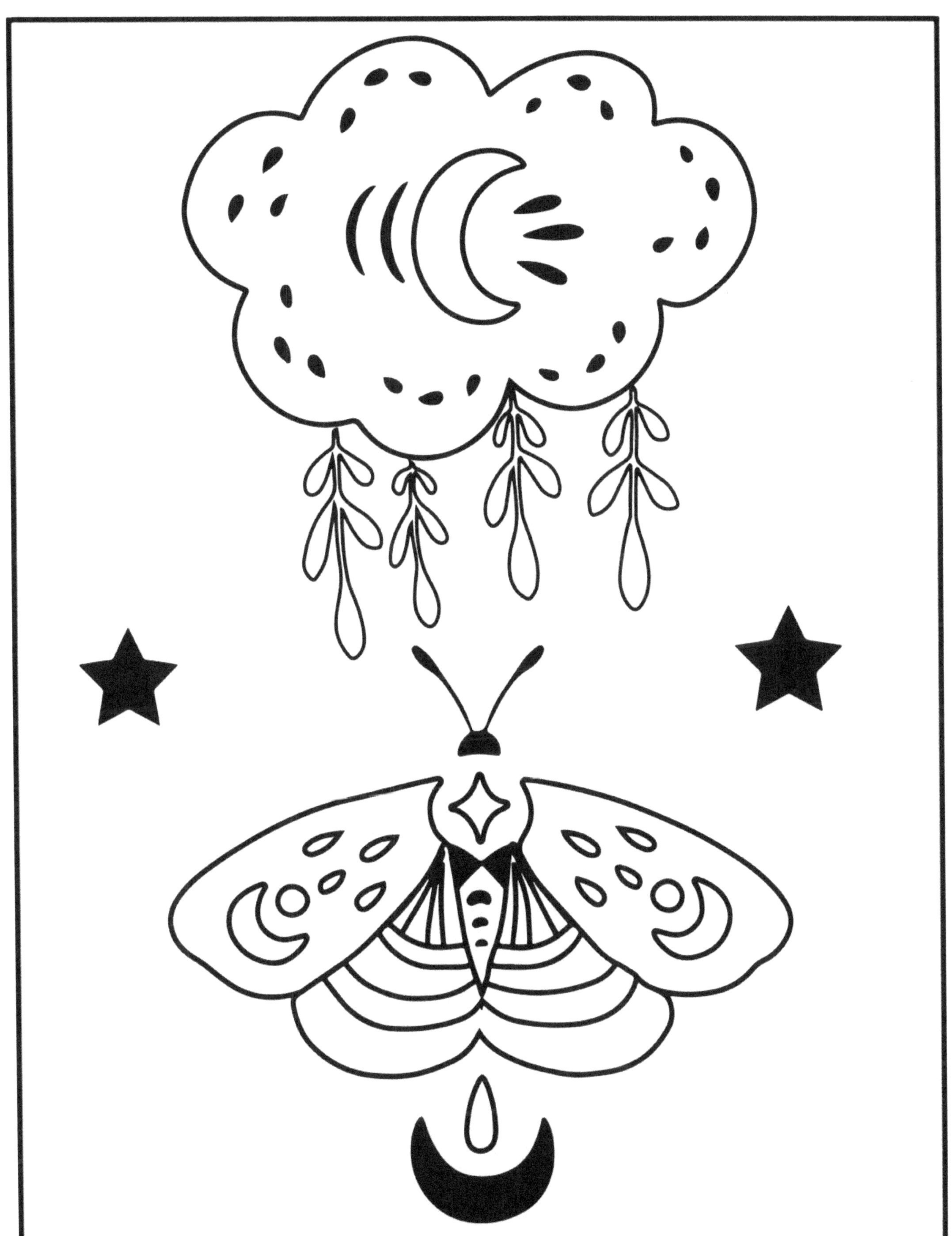

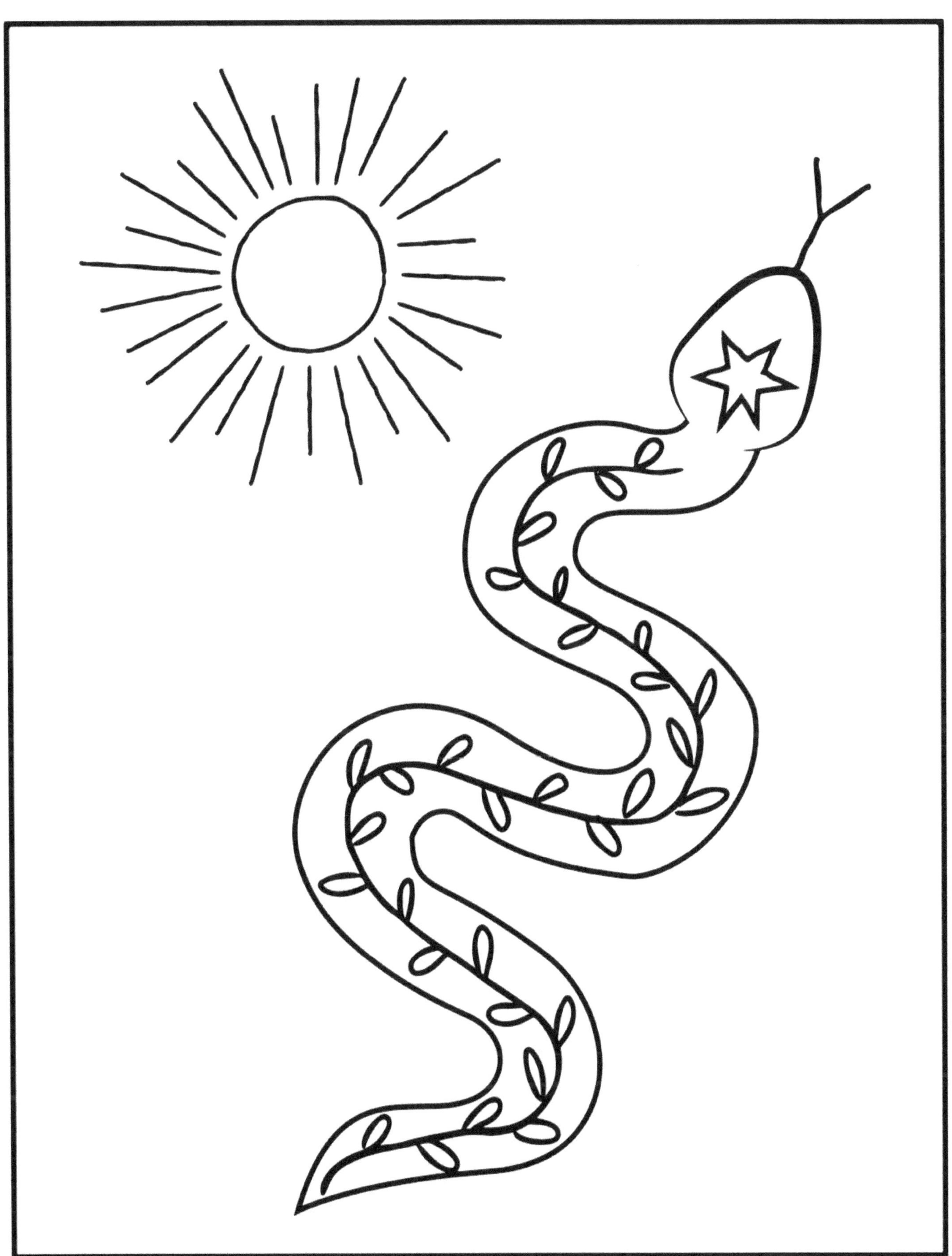

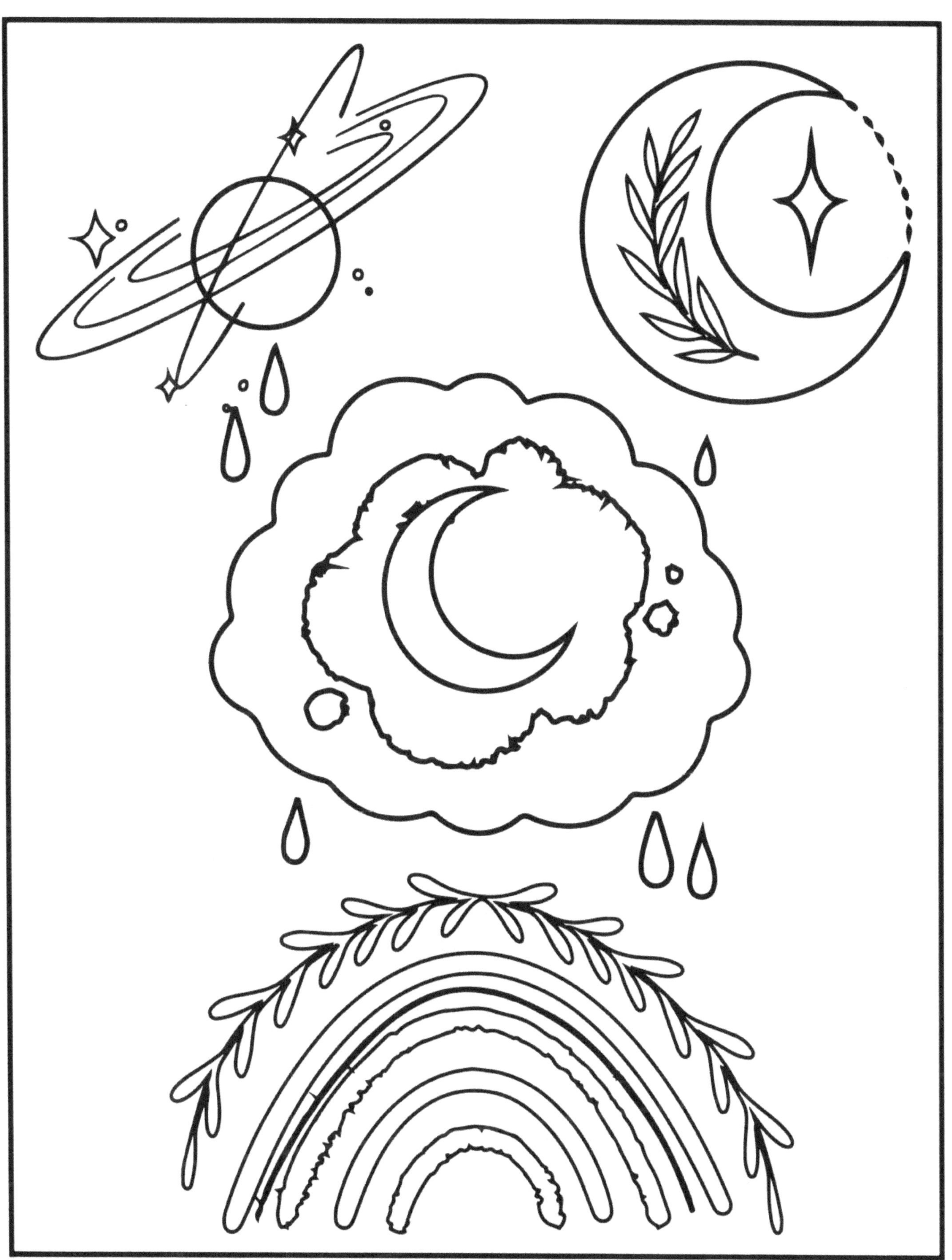

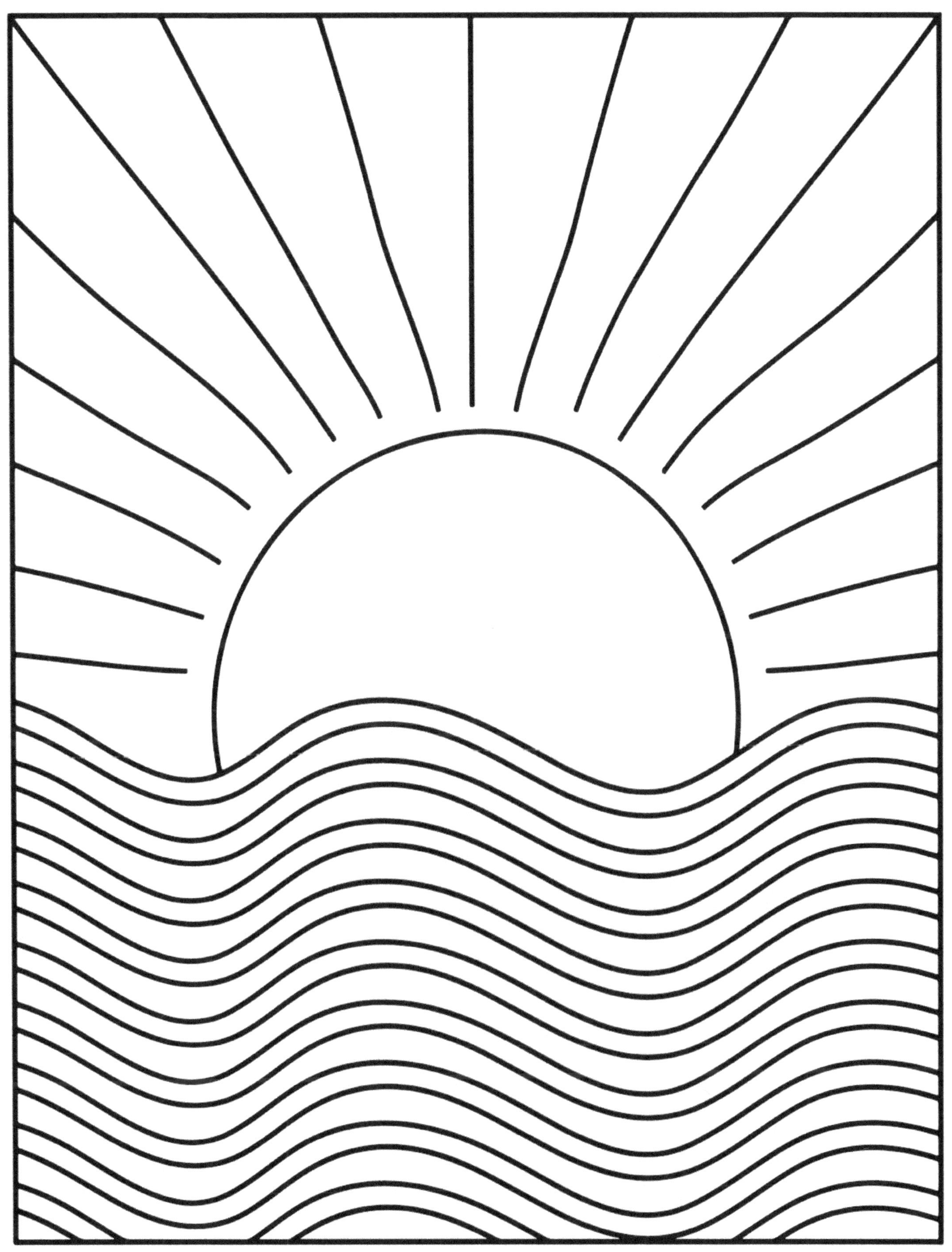

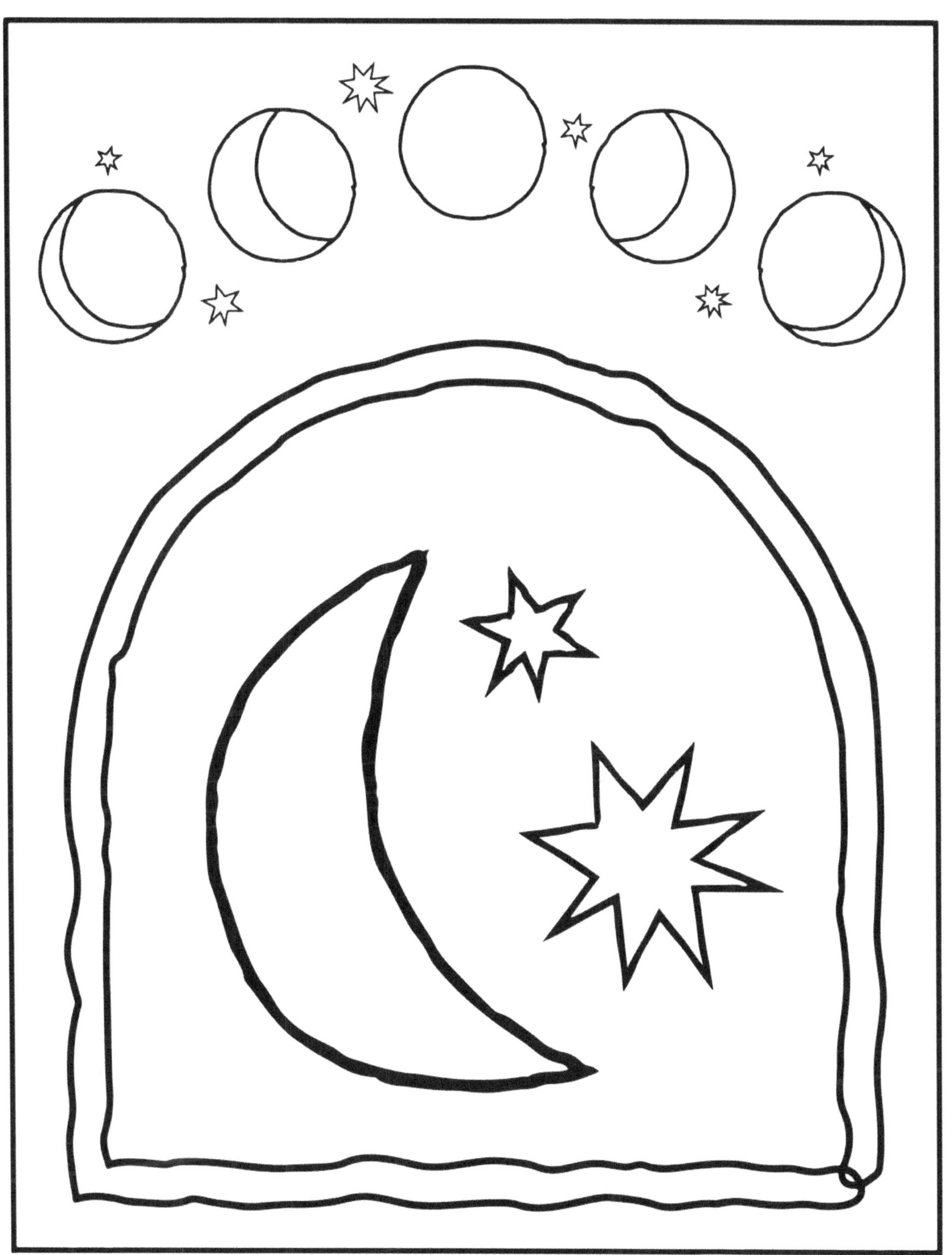

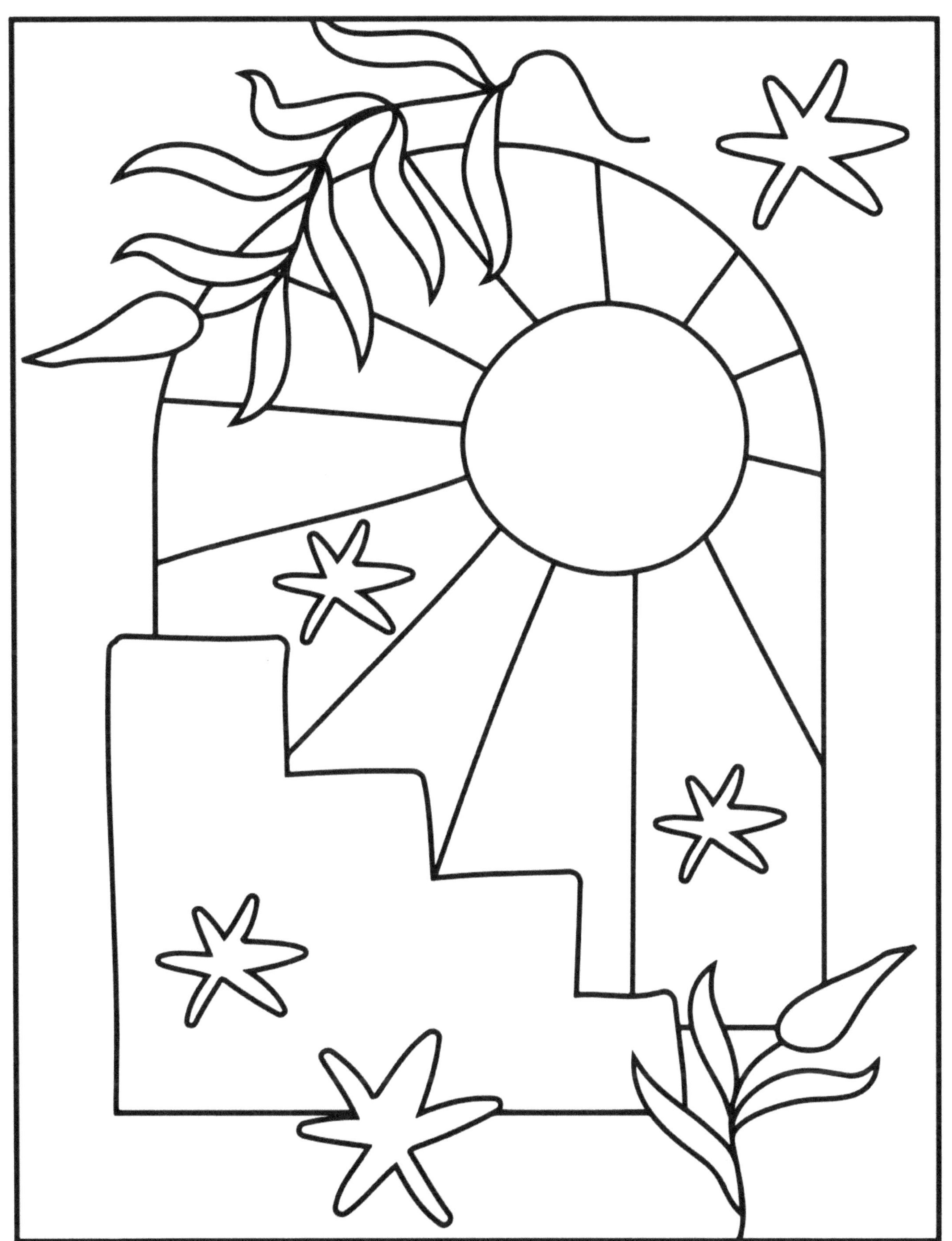

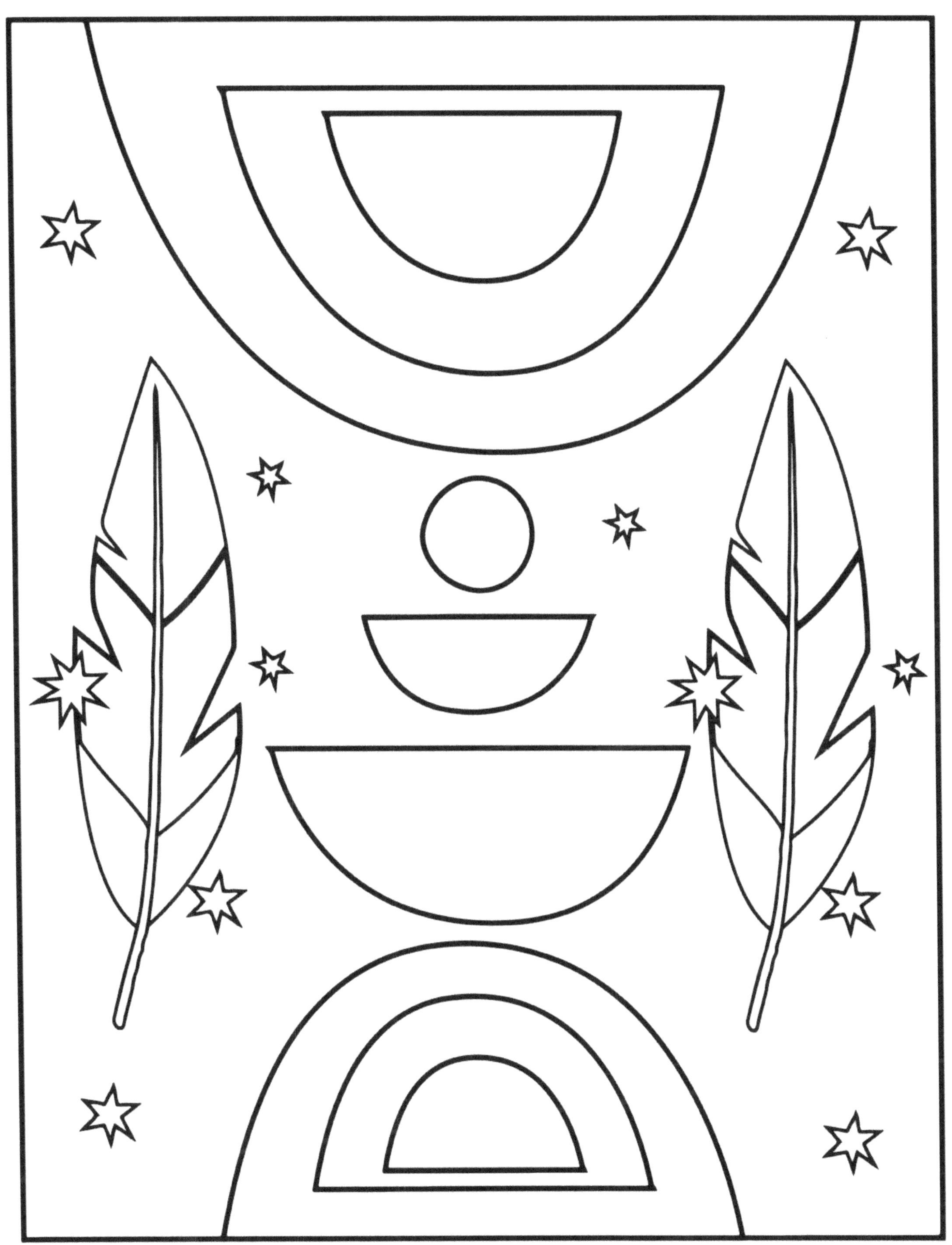

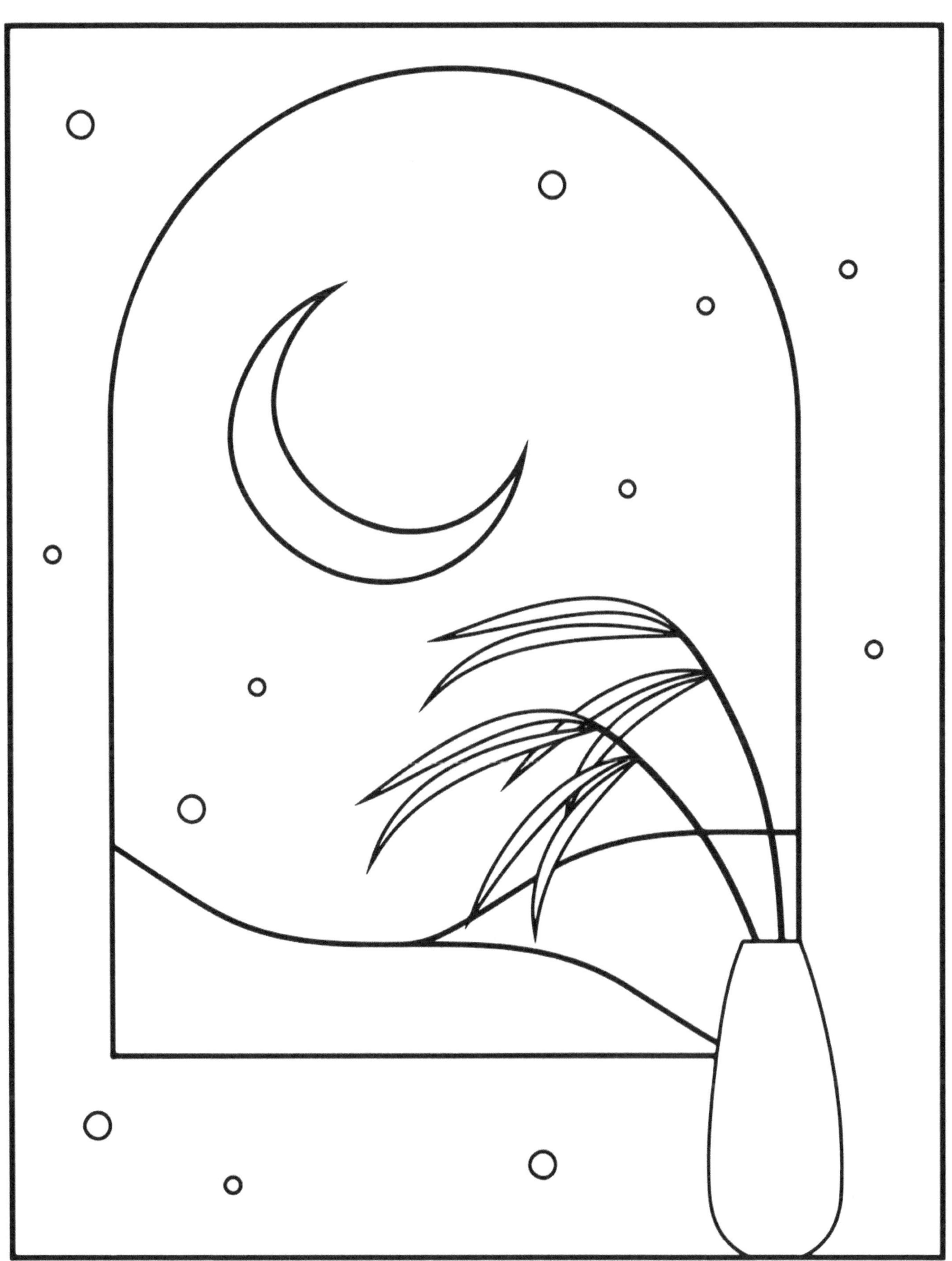

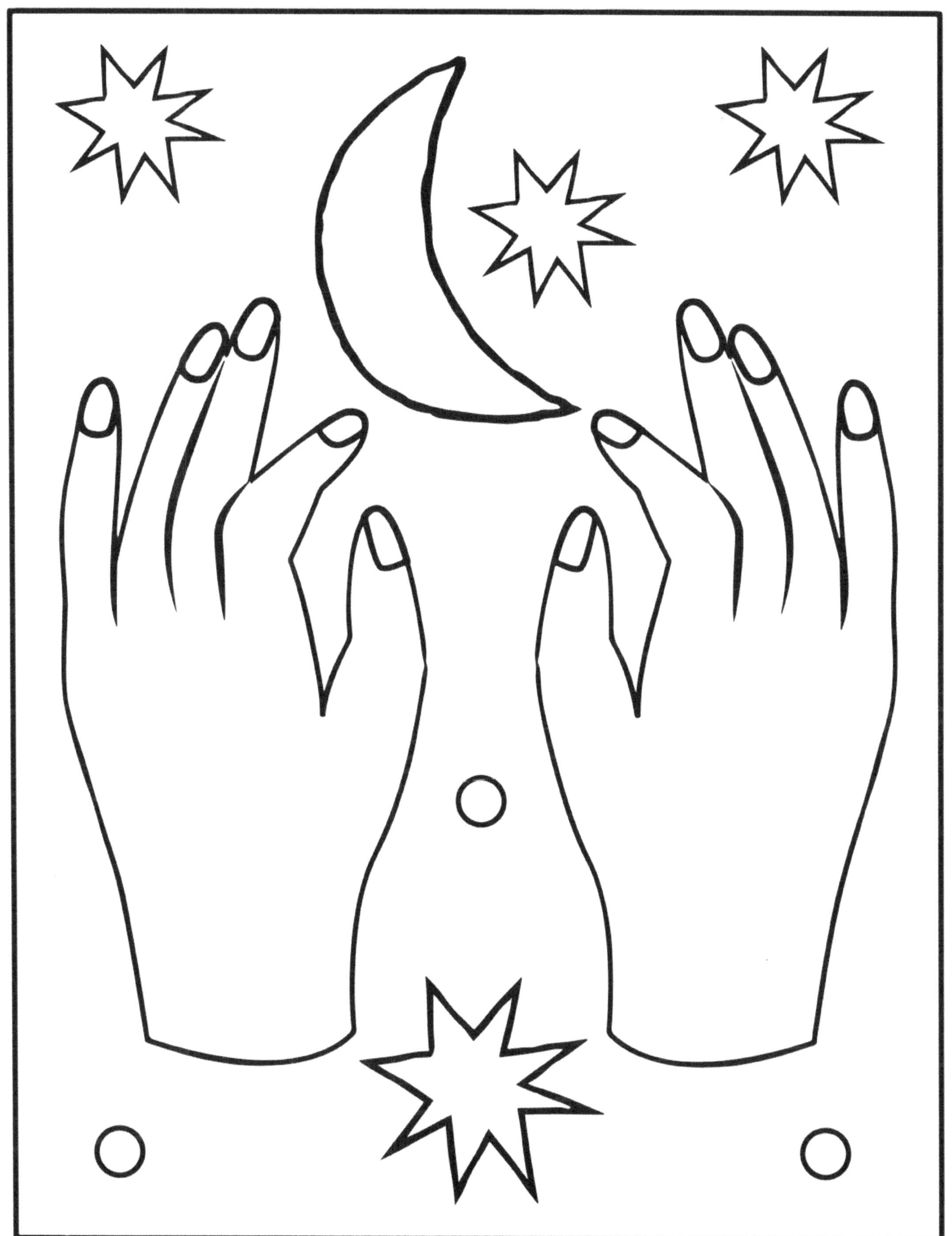

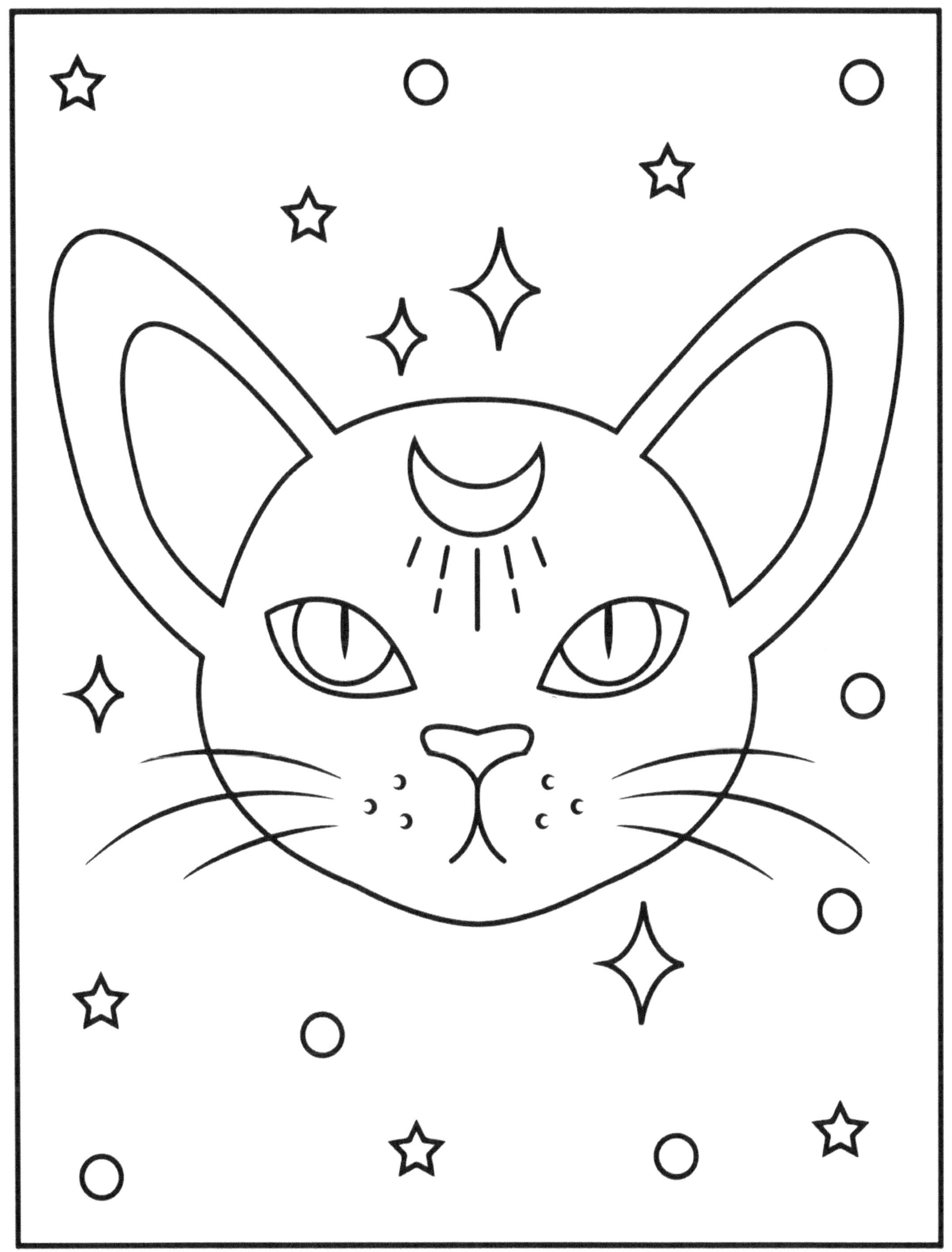

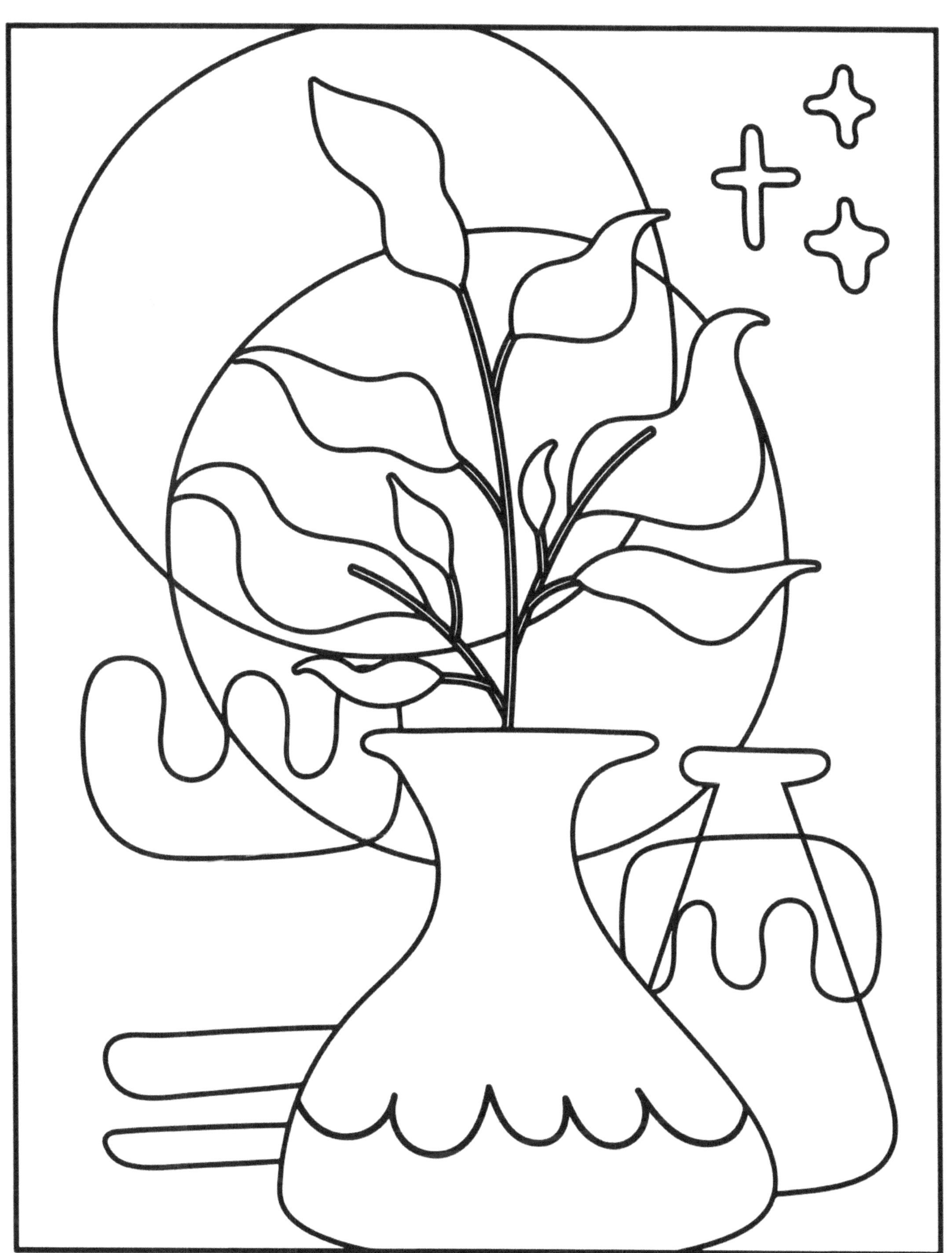

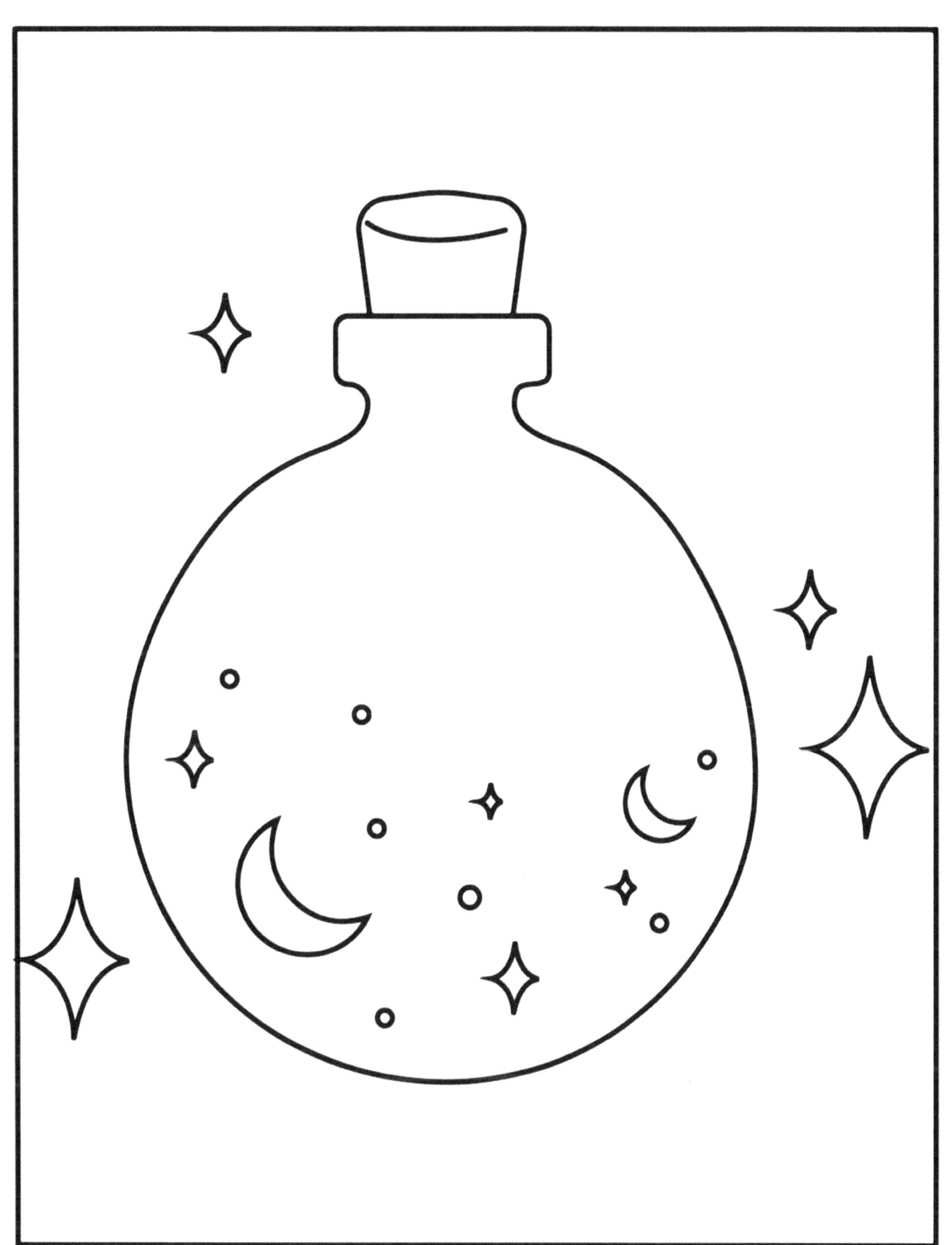

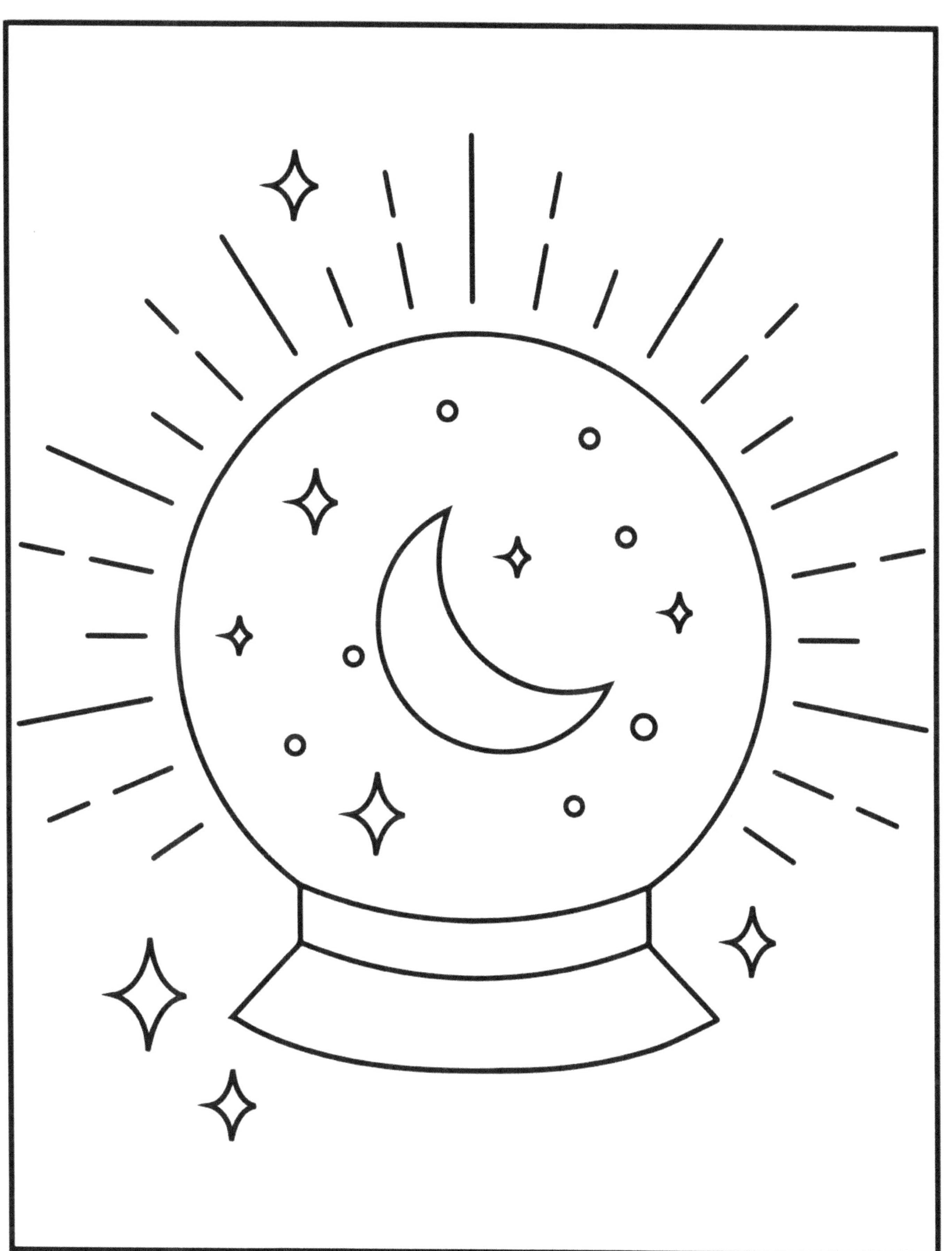

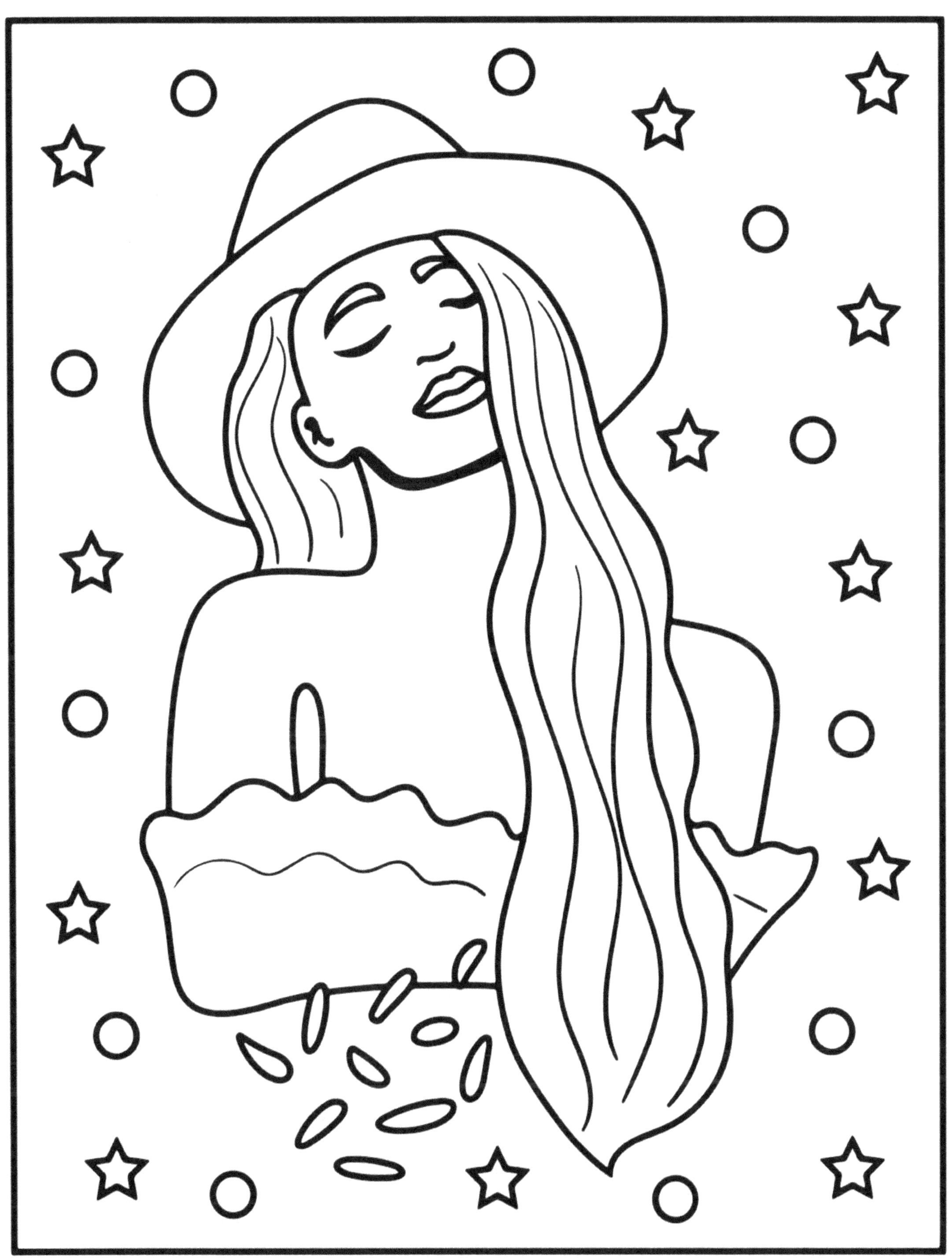

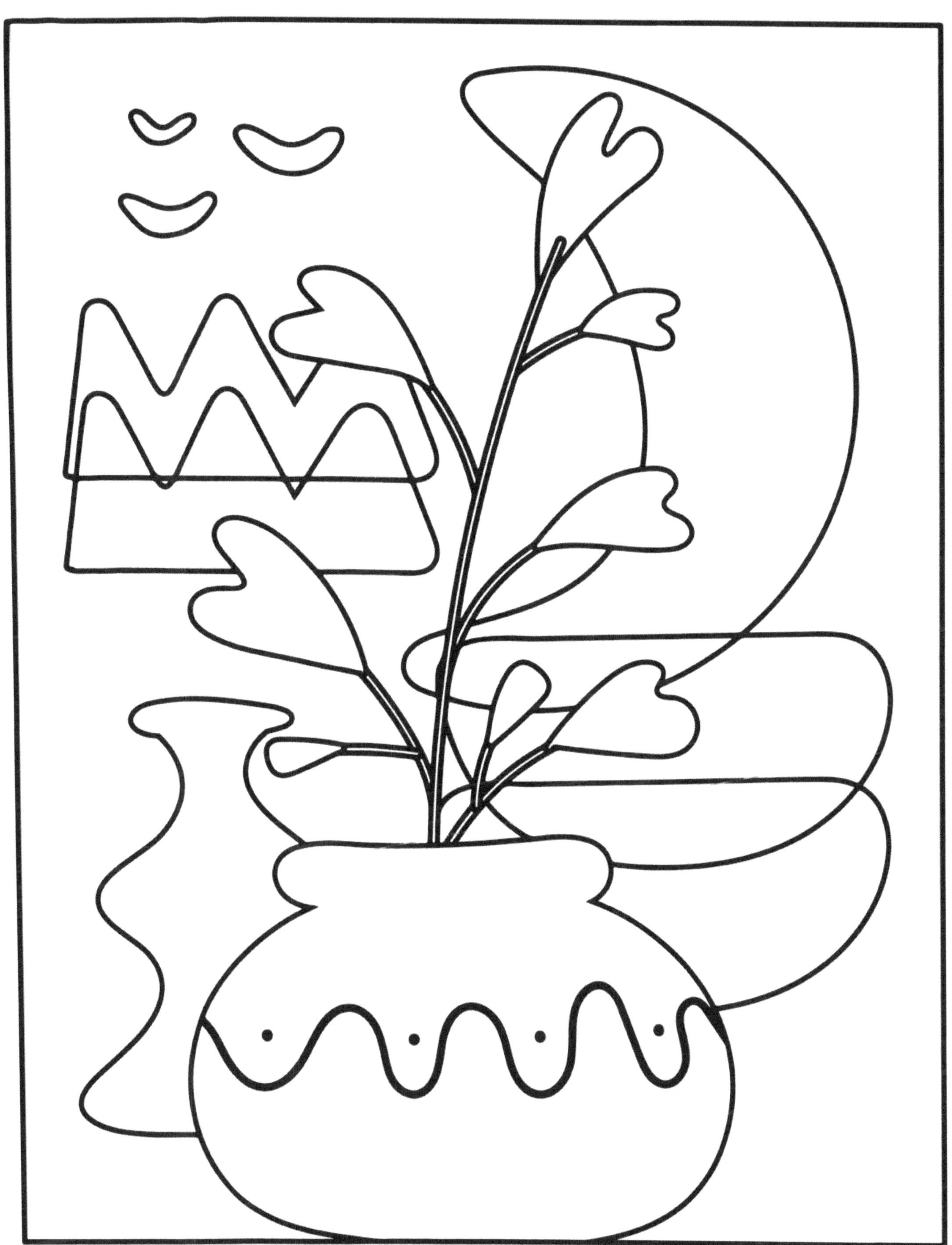

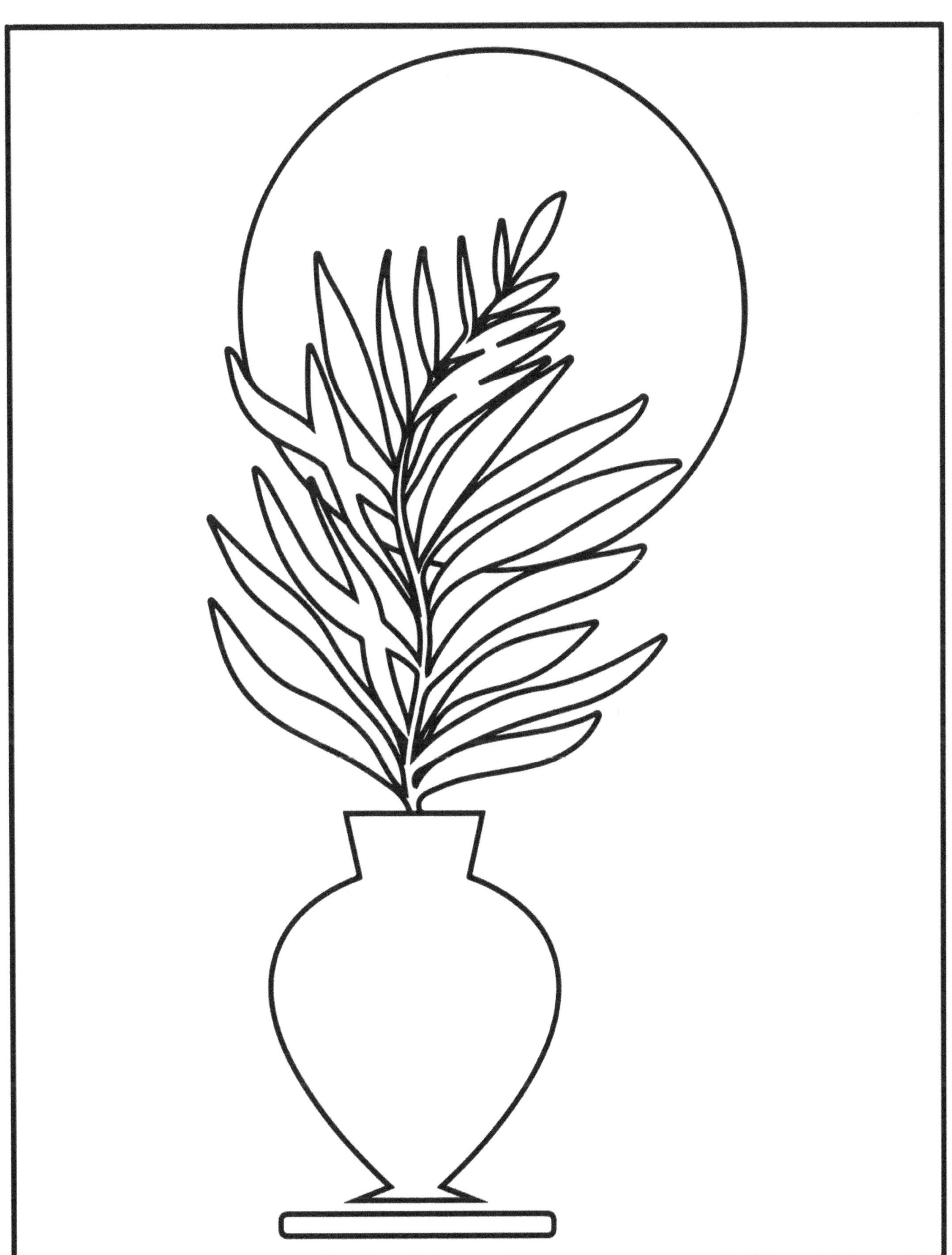

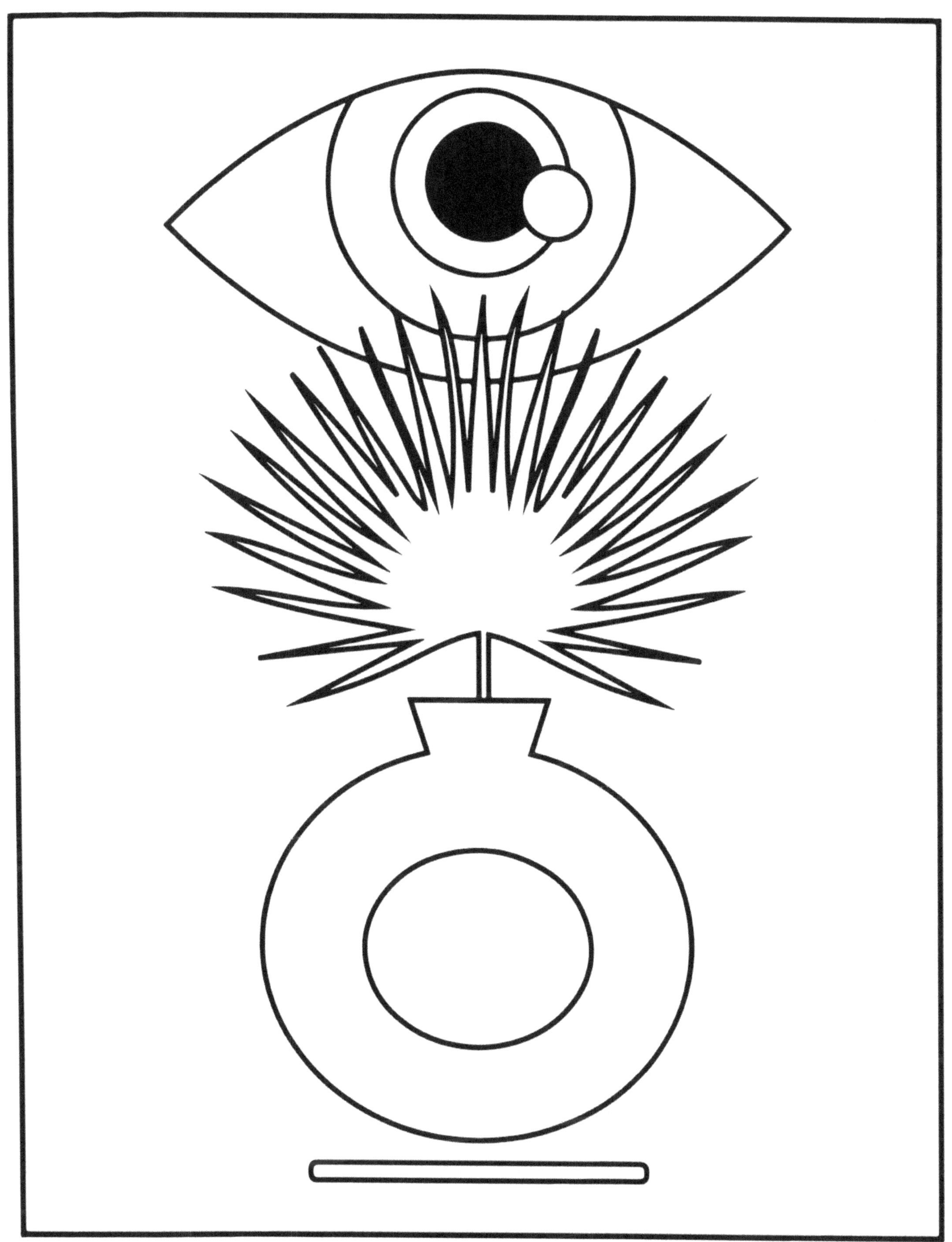

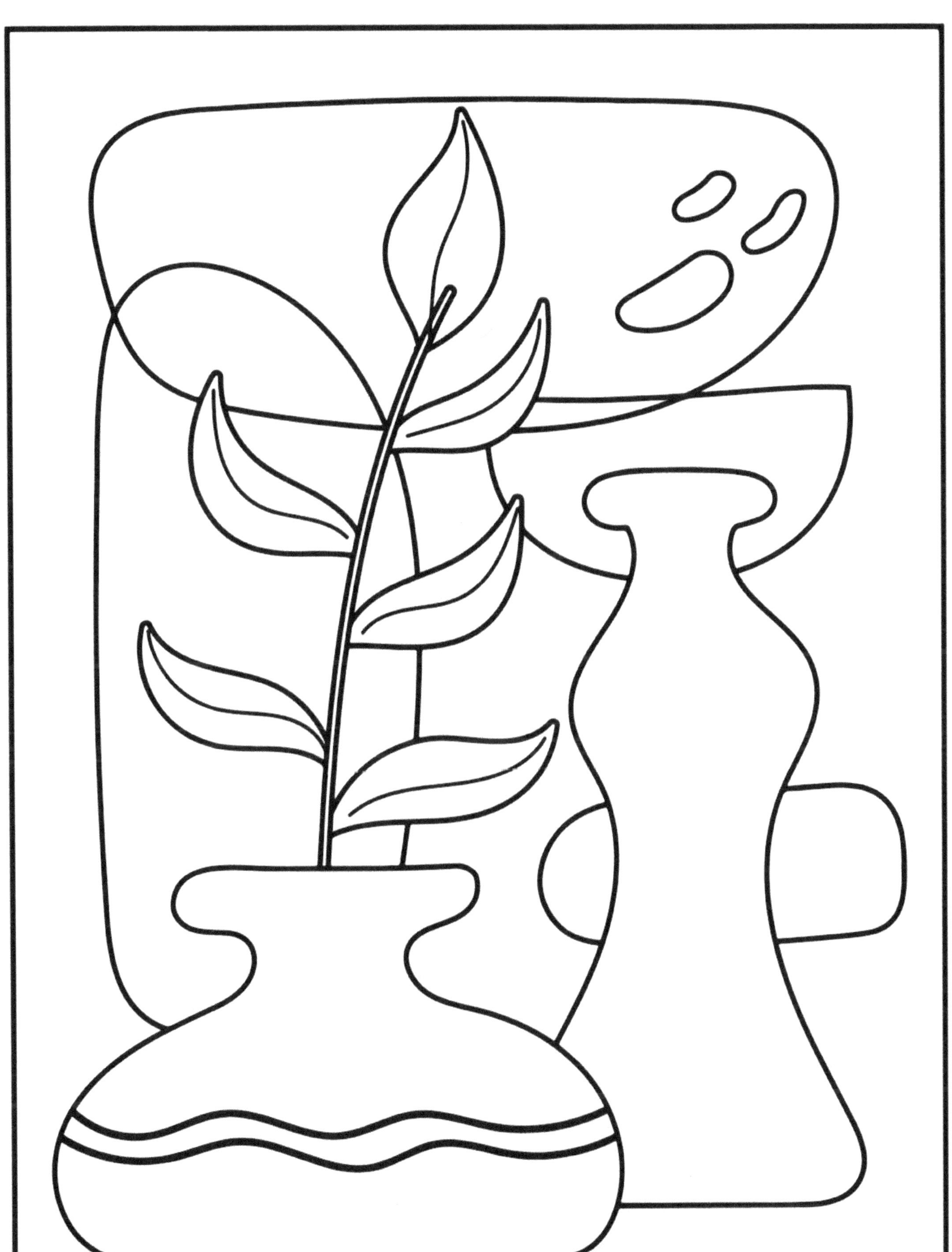

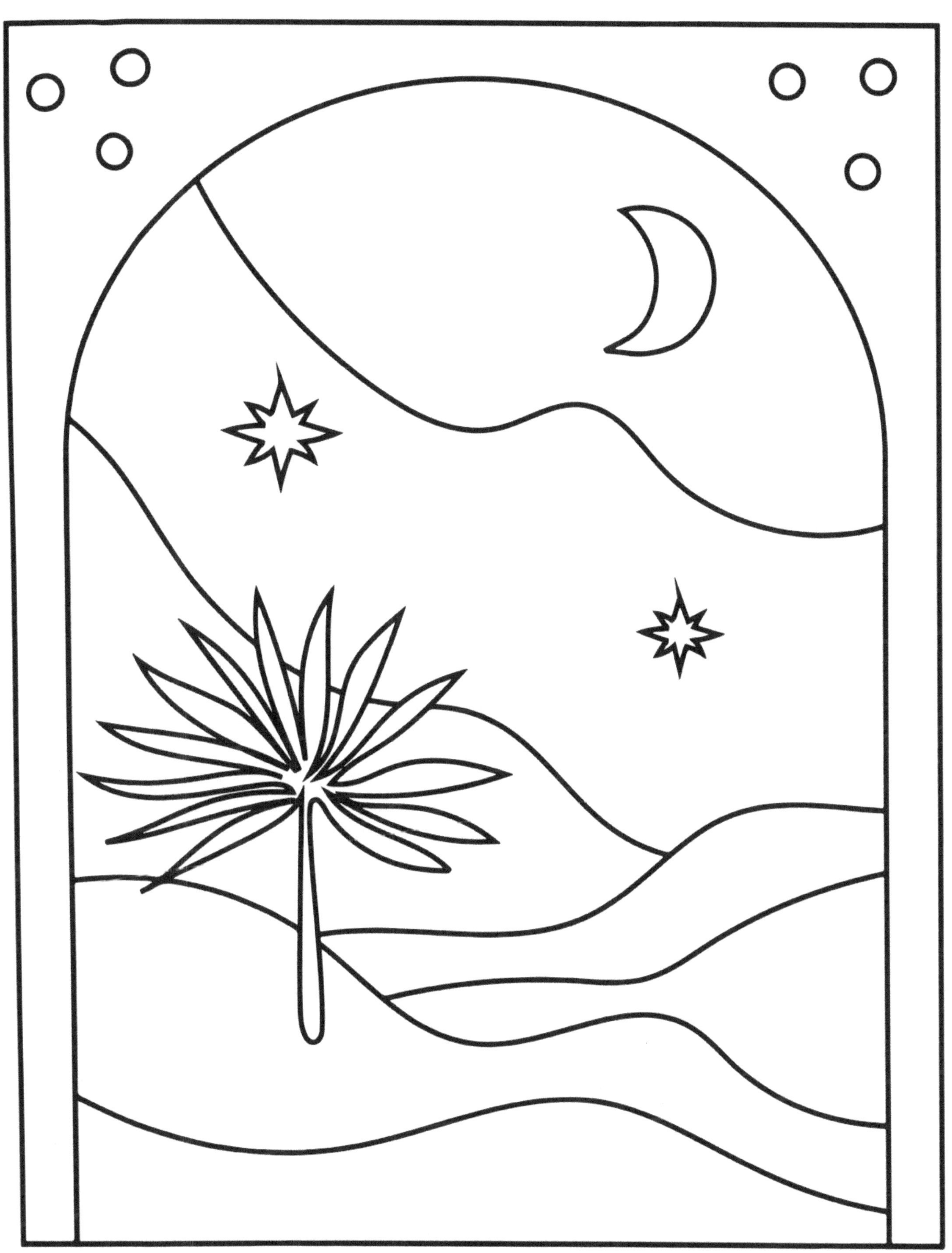

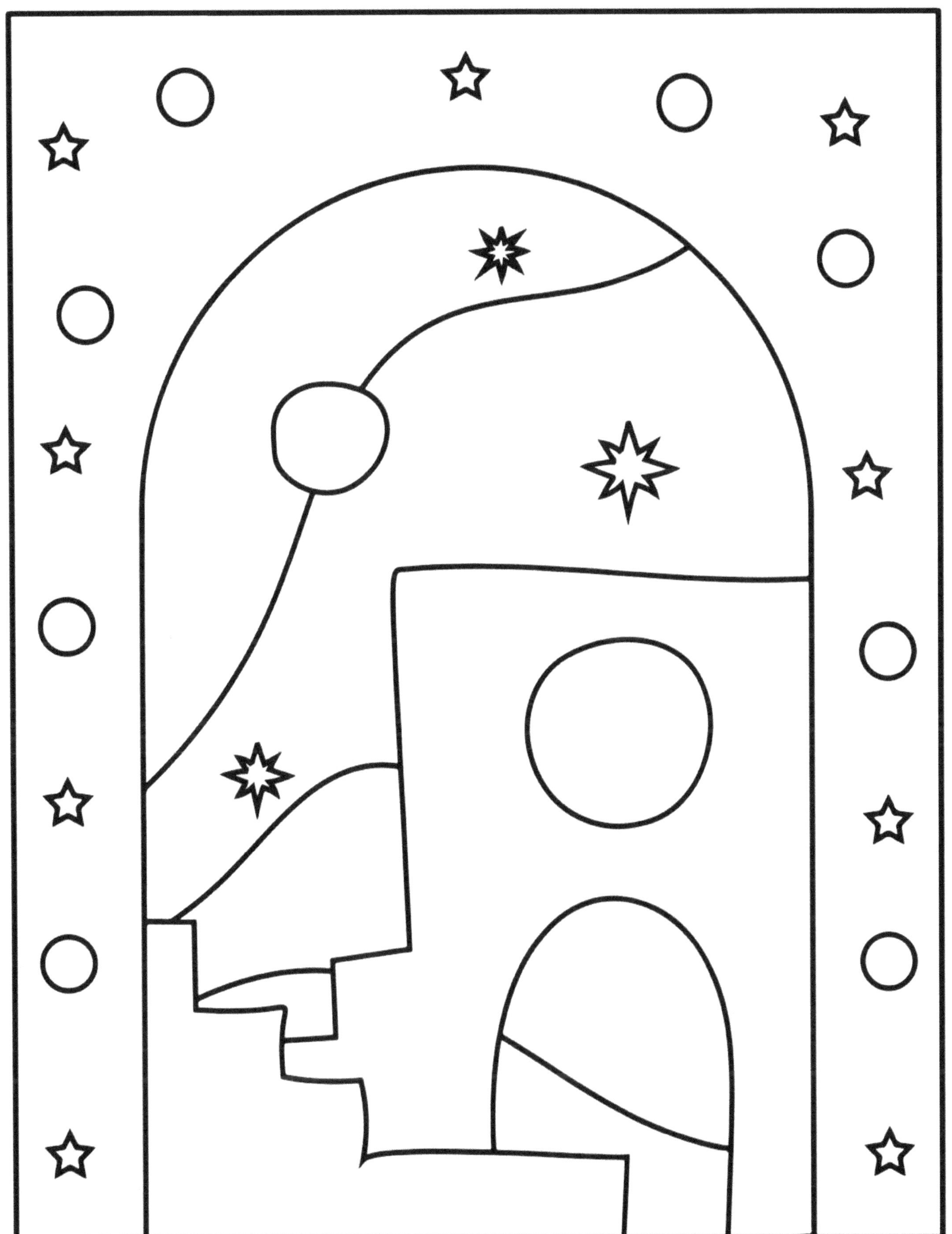

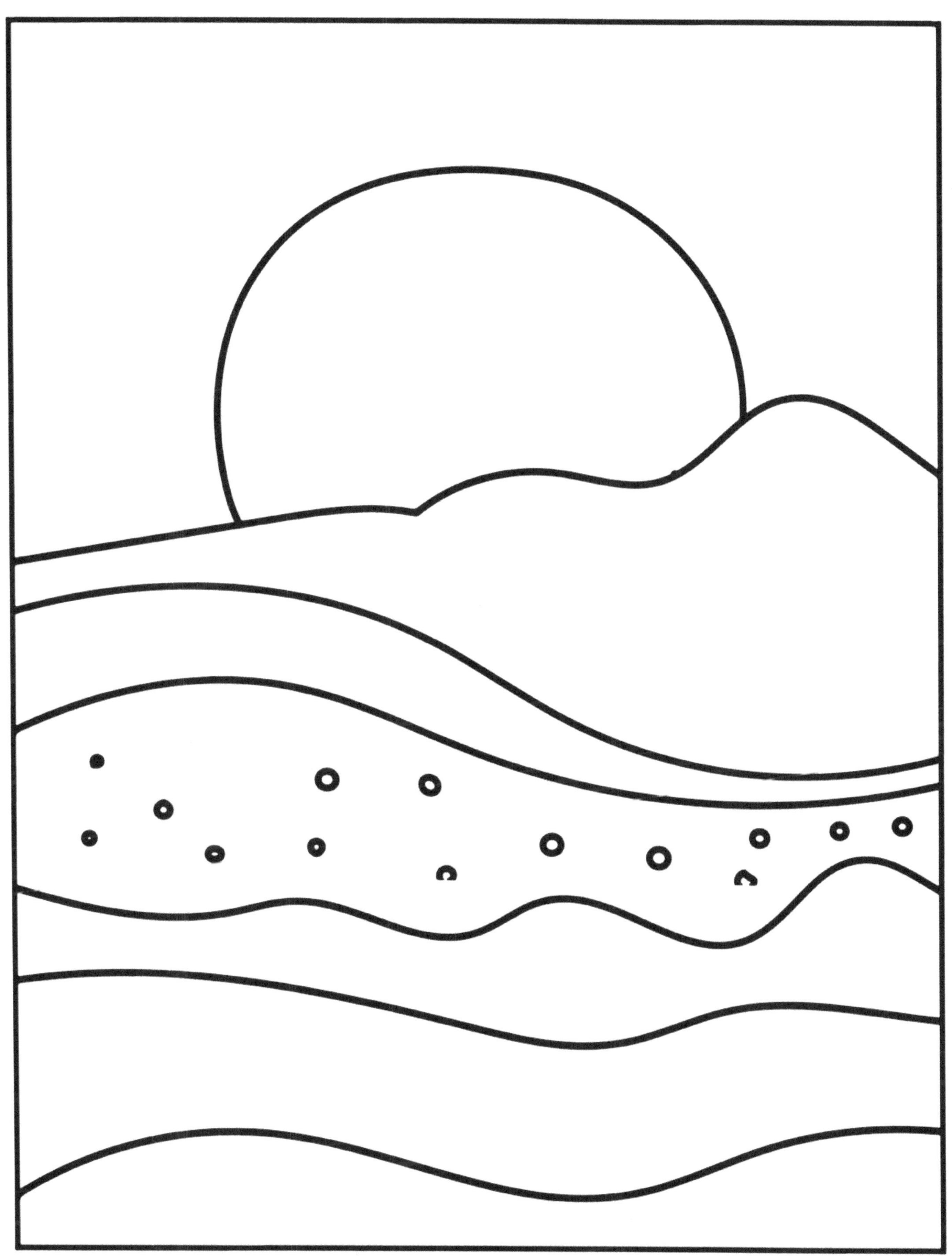

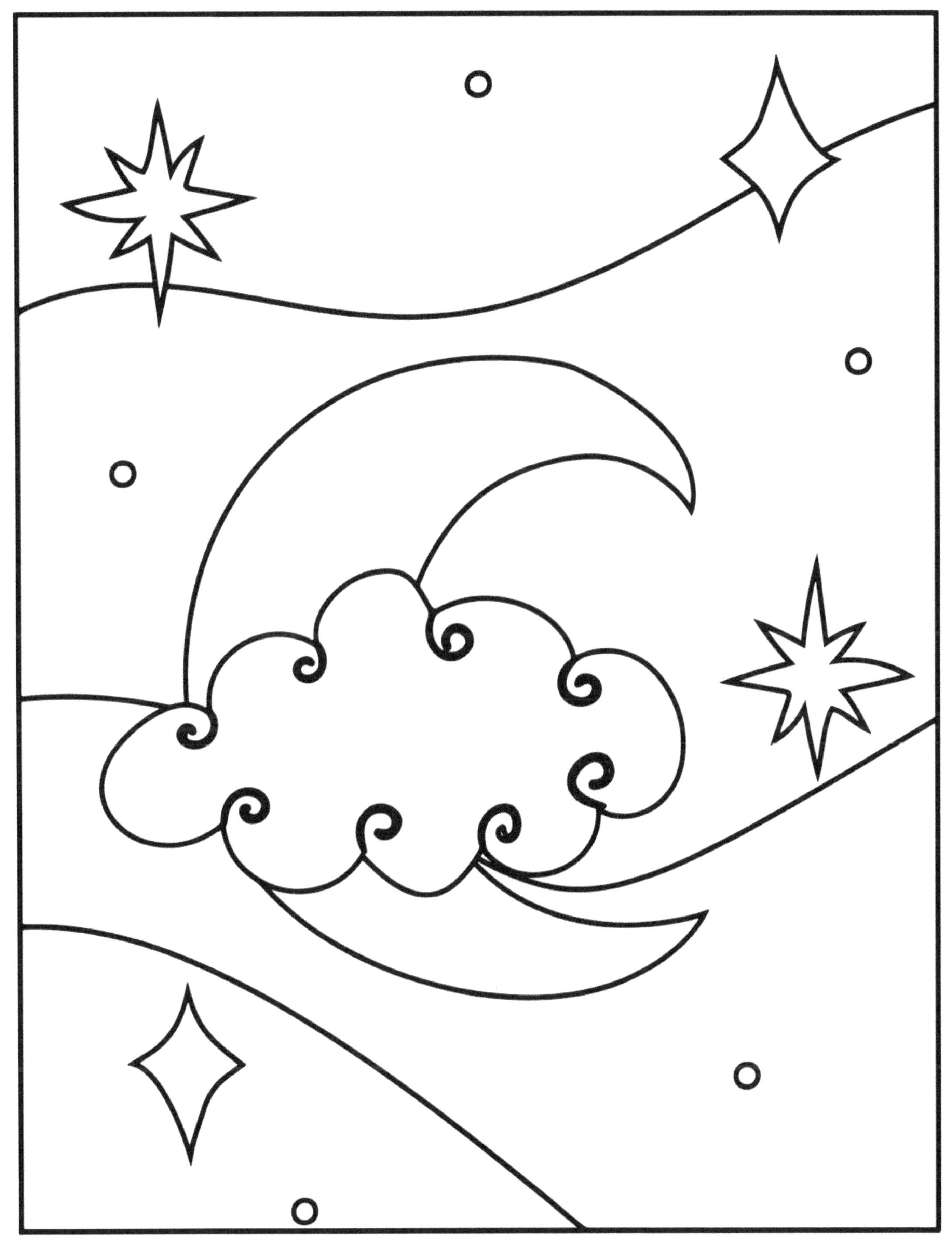

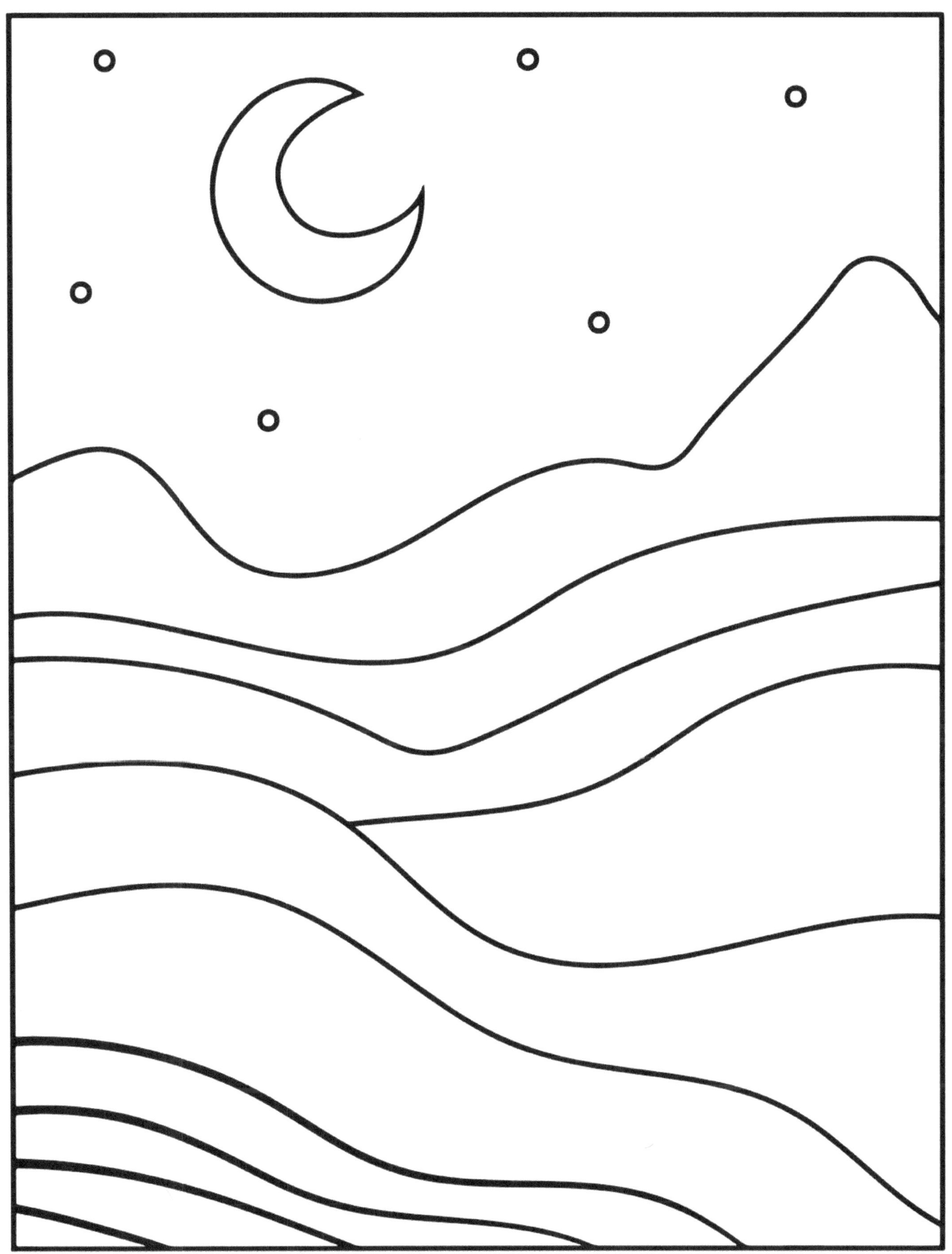

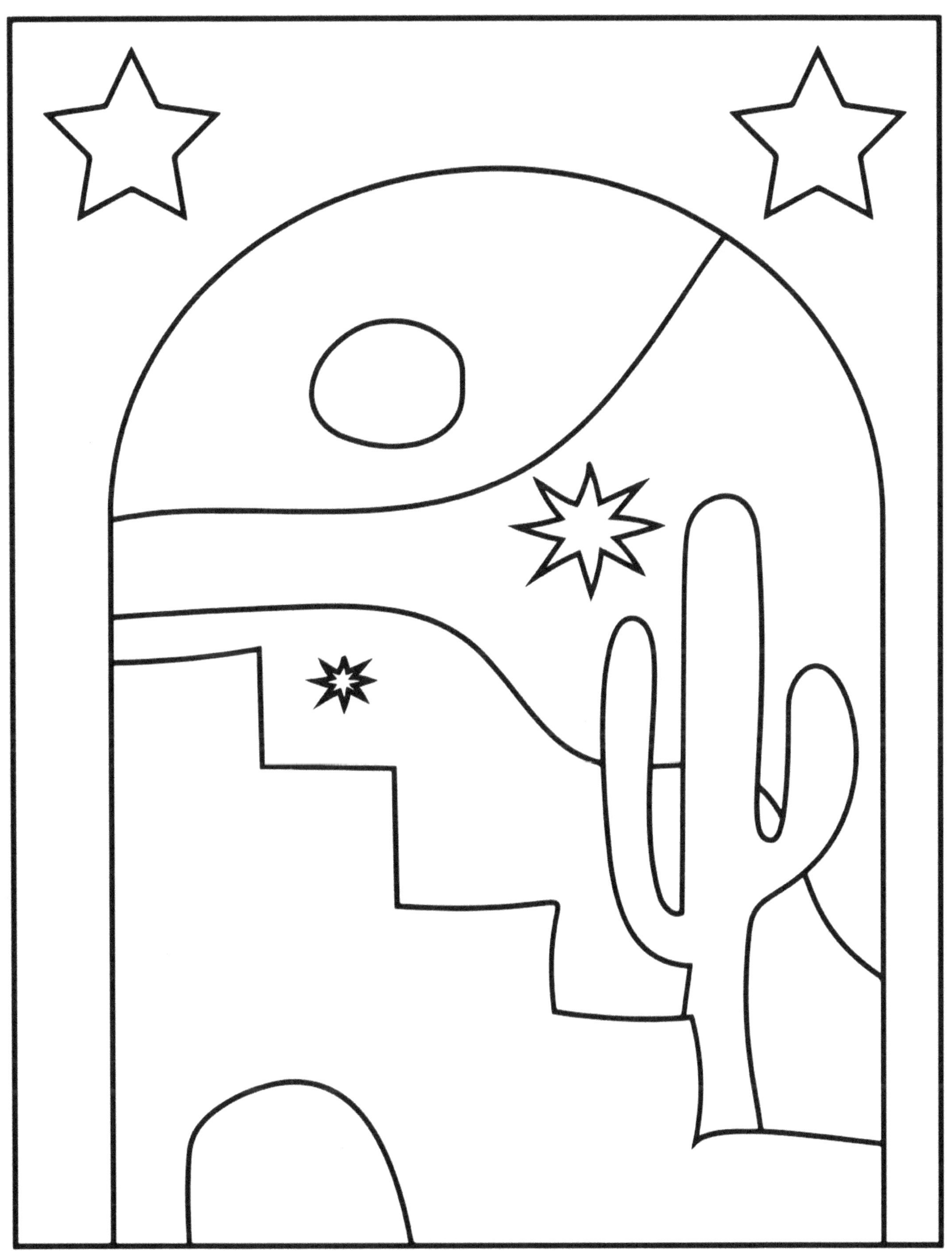

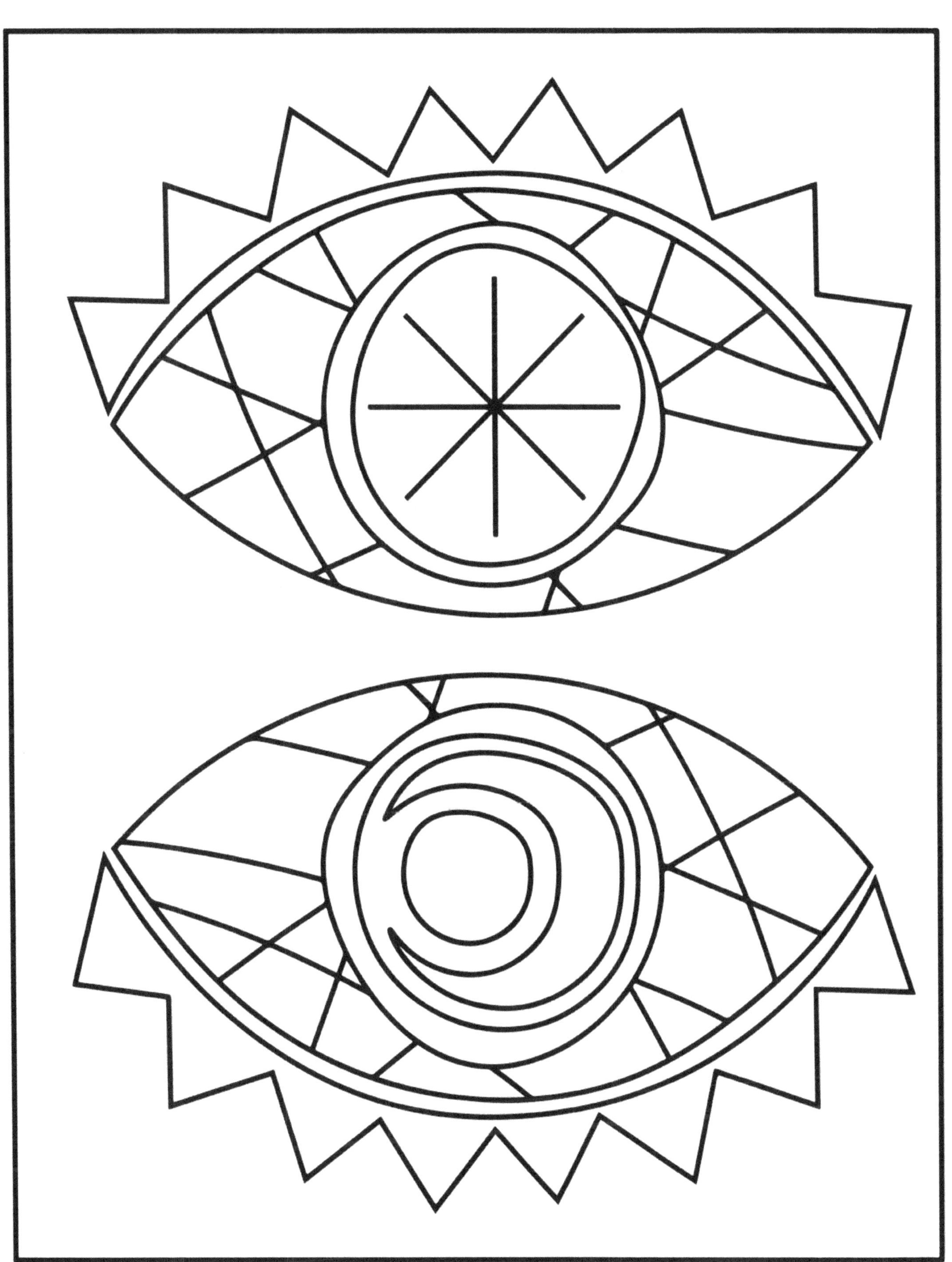

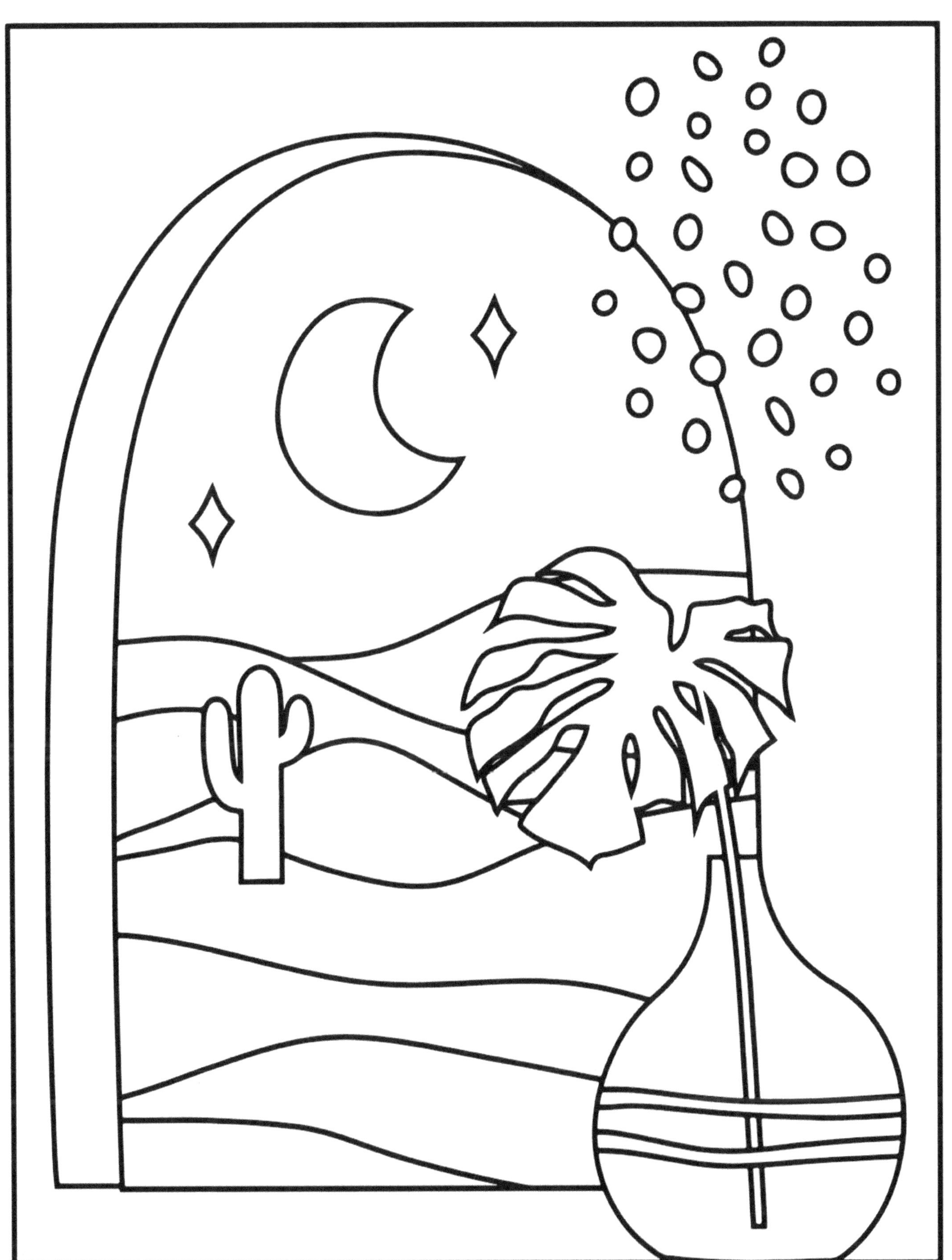

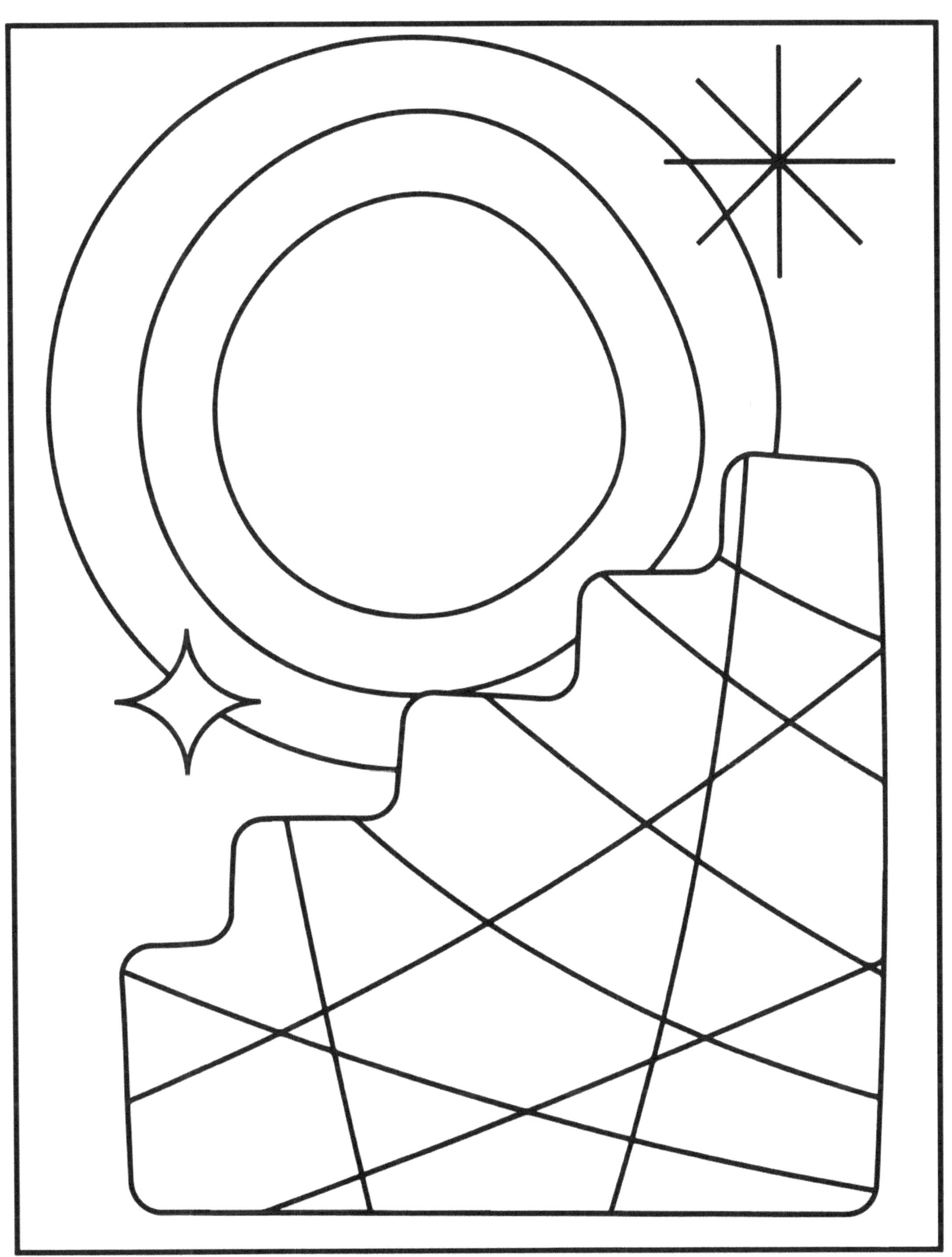

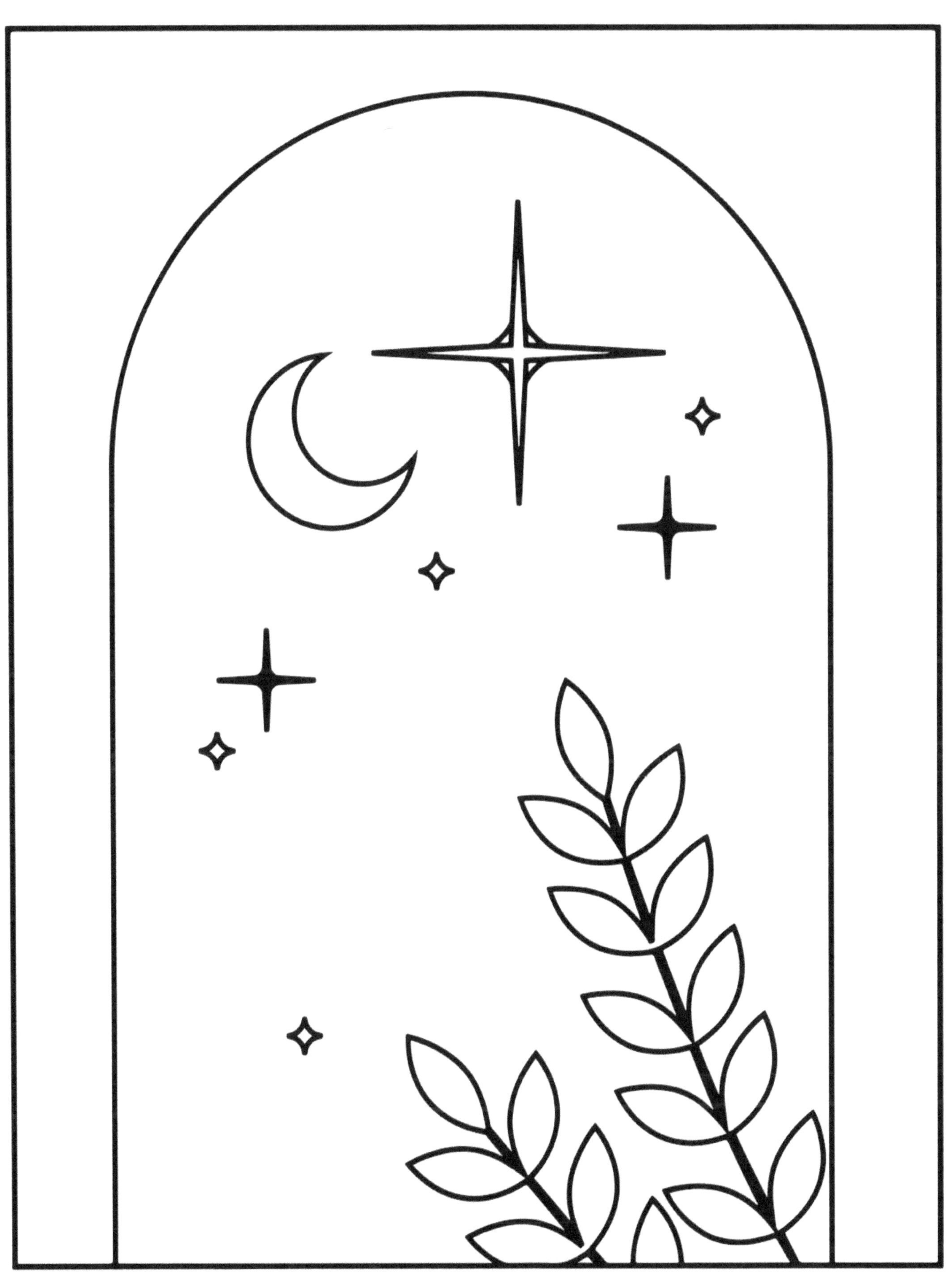

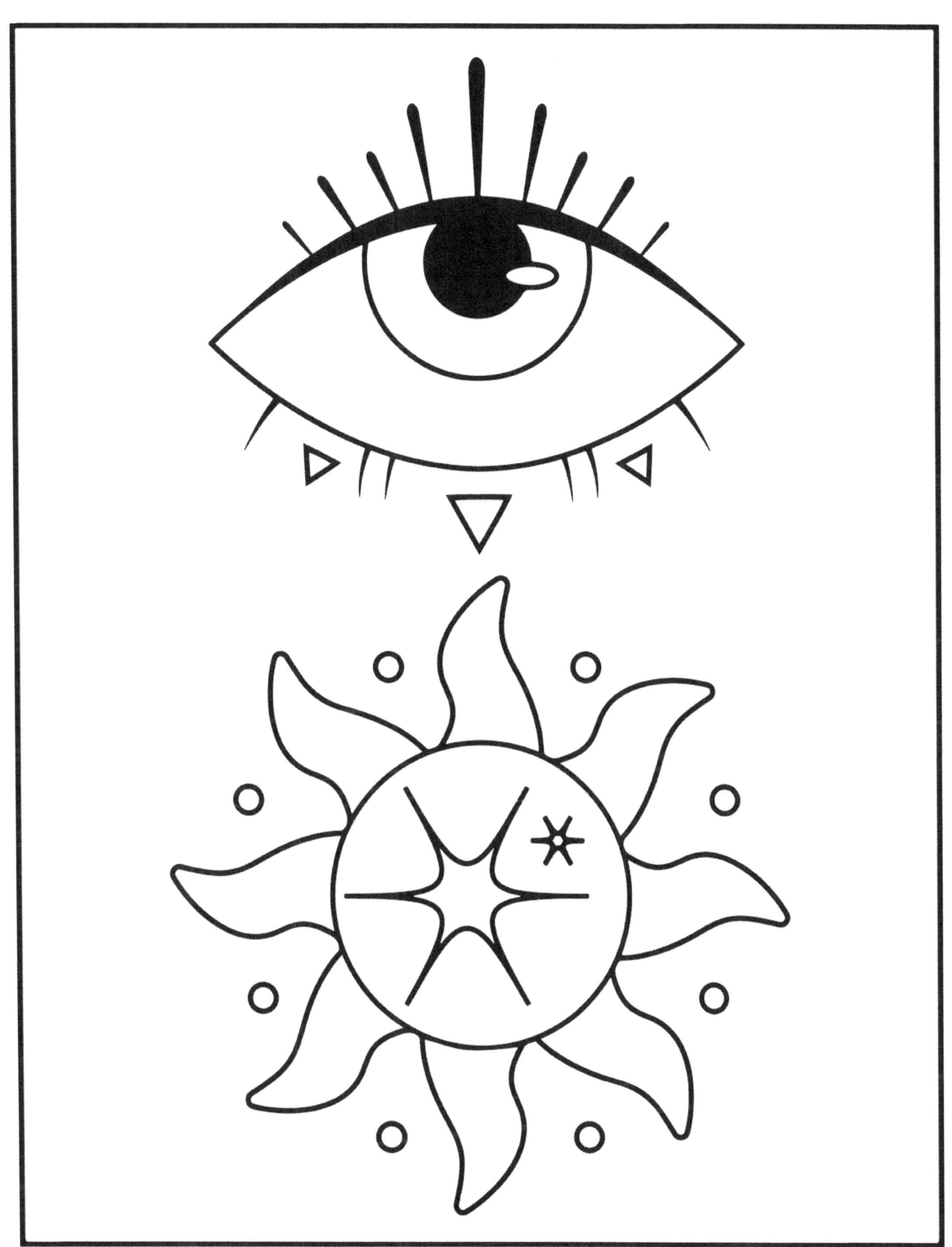

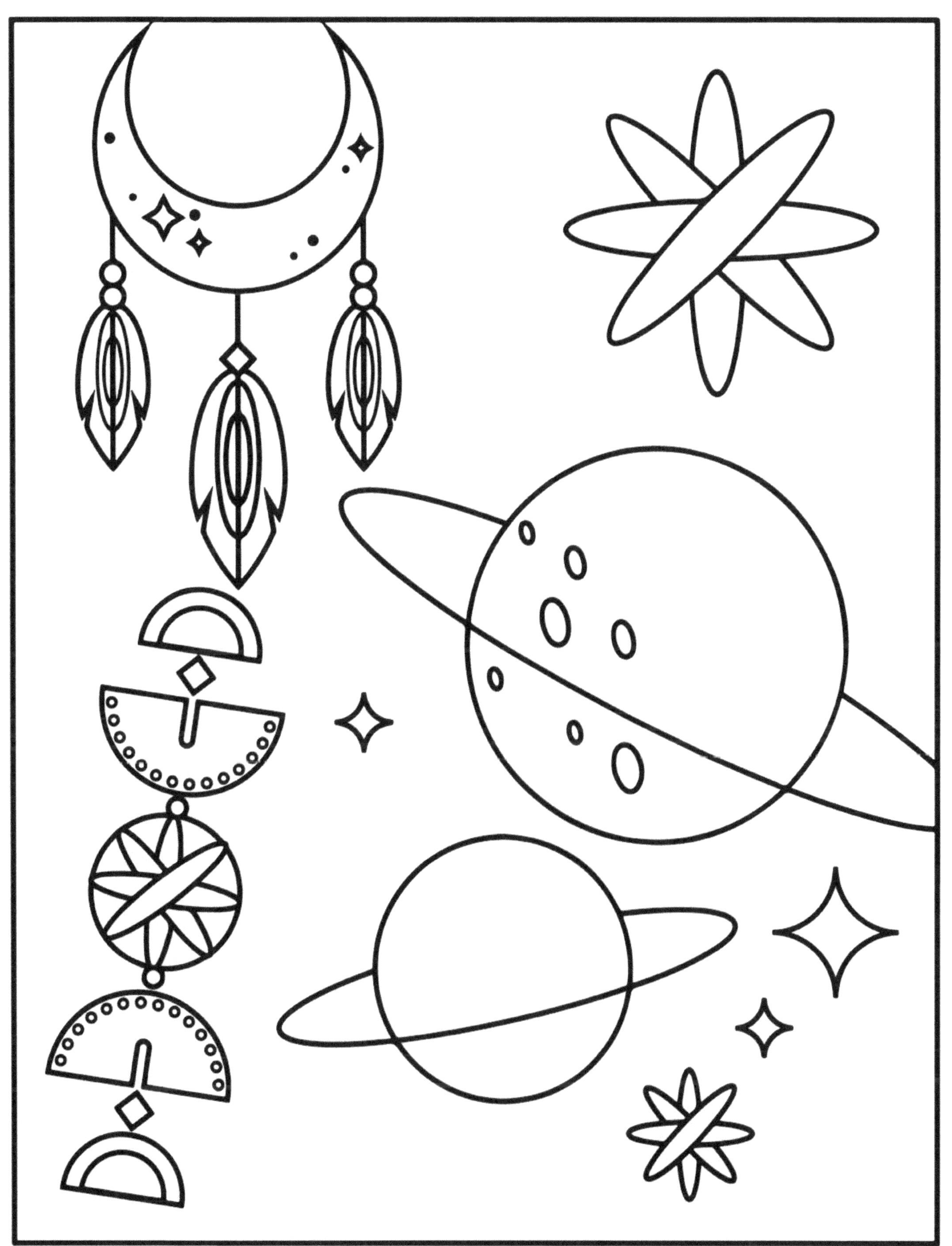

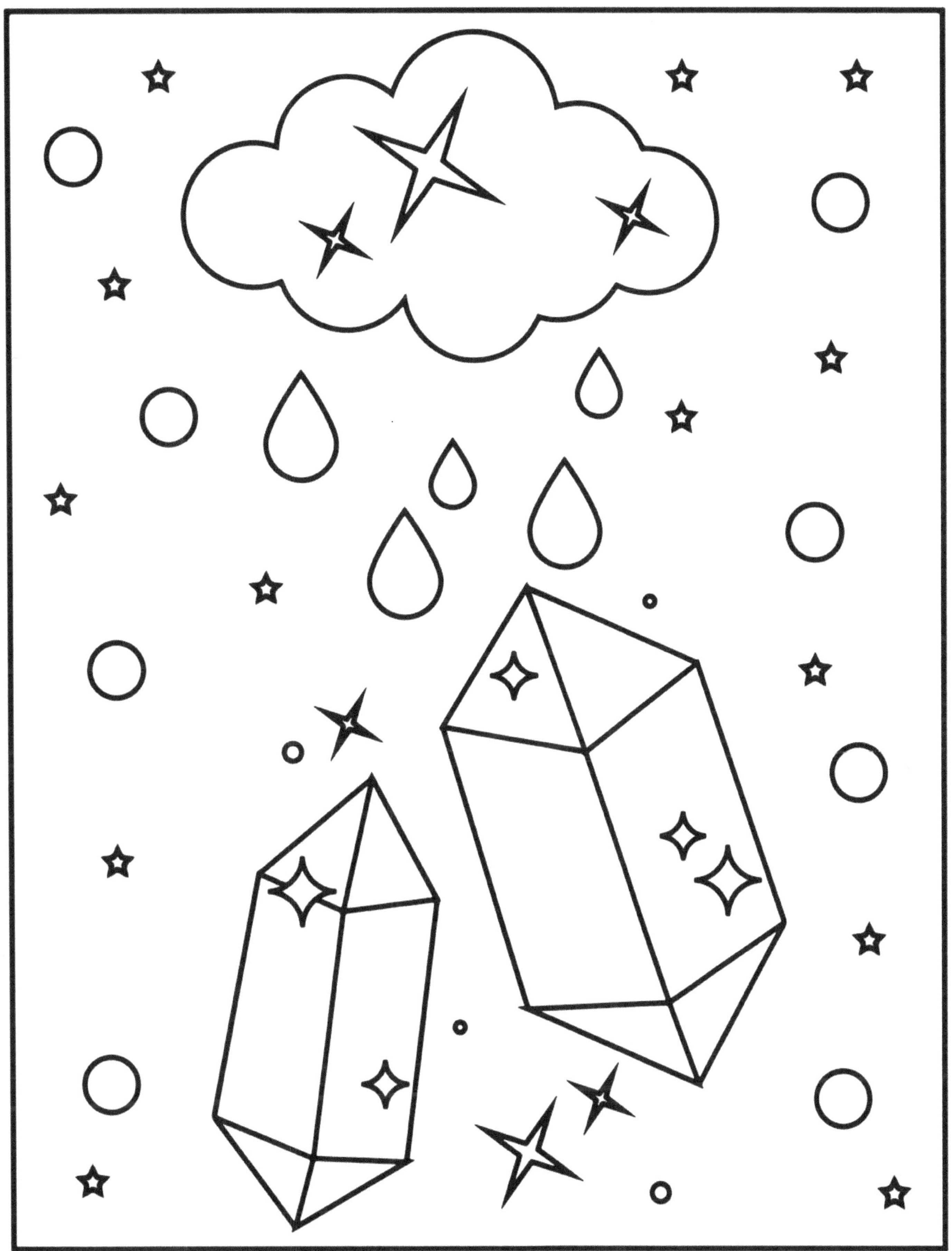

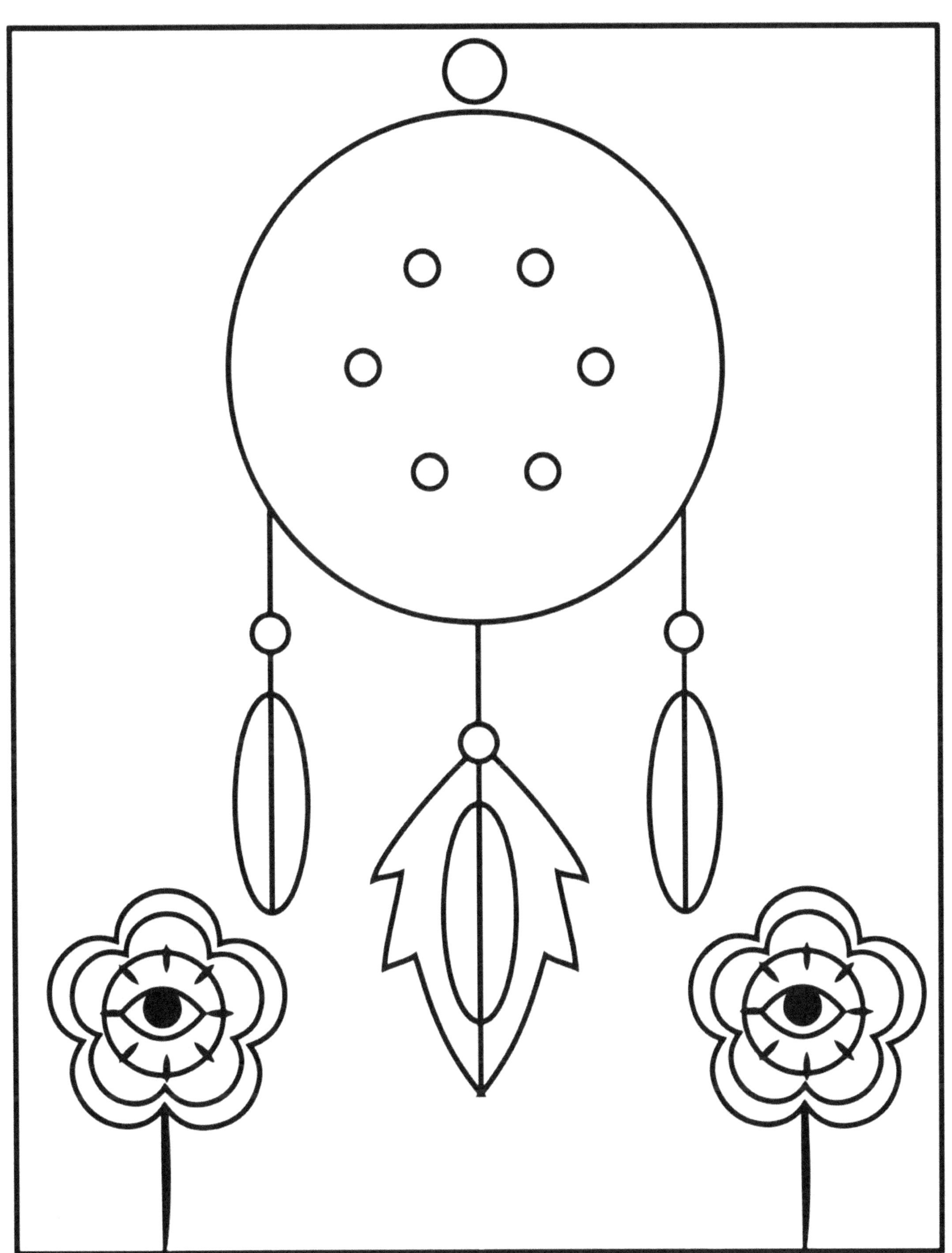

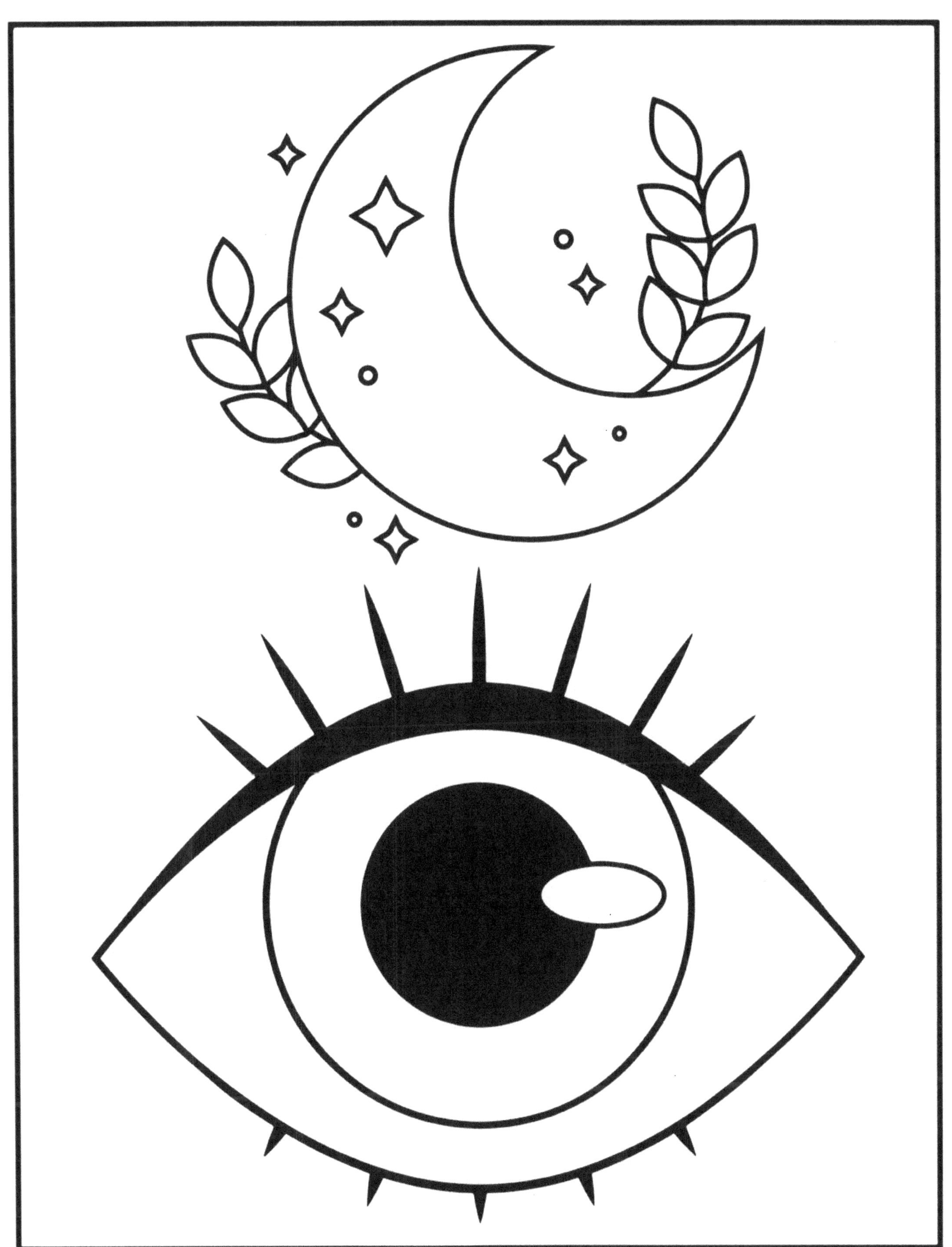

Copyrights 2023 - All rights reserved

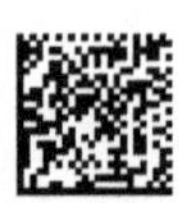